KT-527-259

Down
to
Earth

Gardening Wisdom

Monty Don

DK

Contents

Introduction 6

The Seasons 10

Weather 24

Nature 26

Place 30

Design 32

Walking and Sitting 40

Colour 42

A New Plot 48

The Small Town Garden 54

The Cottage Garden 65

The Exotic Garden 73

A Modern Urban Garden 81

Wildlife Gardening 84

Children 97

Containers 98

Climbers 108

Flowering Shrubs 114

Lawns 117

Weeds 121

Fungus 128

Pests 130

Compost 140

Tools 144

Planting 148

Growing 152

Pruning 158

Food 166

Grow your own Veg 172

Grow your own Herbs 180

Grow your own Top Fruit 186

Grow your own Soft Fruit 192

Names 200

The Months 202

January 204

February 208

March 215

April 220

May 225

June 229

July 235

August 240

September 245

October 251

November 258

December 261

Index 264

Acknowledgments 272

Introduction

I began 'proper' gardening at about seven but had always played in the garden, and at its best, gardening for me still has exactly the same allure that going out to make camps did as soon as I was old enough to run around outside.

But gardening was not always at its best. In fact, throughout my childhood I saw it as another chore that had to be completed in order that I would be free to play in the woods and lanes around the Hampshire village where I grew up. This was chalk country and I now realise that the vegetation of that very particular geology shaped my world as much as any other aspect of my upbringing. Beech woods, hazel coppice, fields waving with soft green barley and the glassy flints that pocked the chalk defined normality.

Around the same time that I was considered old enough to contribute to the onerous business of running a large garden, I was sent away to boarding school. Although a mere 18 miles away, the soil there was thin, sandy and very acidic. From it grew rhododendrons, heather and pines. My homesickness was as much a deep longing for the chalk landscape of my village as for my family.

But gardening came to me when I was about 17. By then I had acquired – by default – a working knowledge and could grow vegetables, make compost and keep the place looking fairly tidy.

One day in early spring I was preparing the ground for sowing carrots when I was filled with an ecstatic sense of being exactly where I wanted to be, desiring nothing but this completely fulfilled moment. Fixed somewhere between simple happiness and mystical ecstasy, this sense of completeness in the garden has never really left me.

That night I dreamt that my hands grew deep down into the chalky loam and took root. I awoke refreshed and knowing absolutely that all my future sustenance and fulfilment would be – must be – rooted in the soil.

But this has always been private and deeply personal. Other than at various stages as a student when I worked in France and England to help finance my studies, I have never earned my living as a gardener. I am an amateur and speak only from knowledge gained from private study and over 50 years of personal experience. I will admit to being completely infatuated with gardening and obsessively studying, with a large library that I refer to constantly. That sense of putting my hands deep into the earth and growing a beautiful garden solely for the pleasure and satisfaction of myself and my family has never left me.

But I believe that all good gardens are as much about the people that make them as the plants growing in them. You are an integral part of your garden. It will not exist without you.

So this book is an attempt to set out and share some of that personal knowledge that I have built up over the years. It is not intended as a text book or a definitive guide. Everything is based upon my own practical experience, combined with the deep sense of meaning that gardening has brought to my own life.

I have visited many gardens all round the world and have learned that gardens have to come from the heart or else they will never reach the head. You have to please yourself first and foremost or else you run the risk of pleasing nobody. And chasing after an ideal 'finish' to a garden is doomed to disappointment. Every garden is a work in progress and is as complete as our lives are today. It changes. Always. It can always get better. It often gets worse. Be part of the change. Be flexible.

The process of making a garden is like a river running through your life. The place stays the same but the water, even on the stillest days, always moves.

I am always being asked for the 'right' way to do things or the 'correct' answer to a horticultural question. It seems we long for experts to dispense information and knowledge from on high that can then be slavishly followed. It really is not like that. Personal experience counts for a lot but the more you learn, the more glaringly obvious it becomes how little you know.

The right answers are few and far between and are nearly always very much less interesting and informative than the right questions. Failure teaches much more than success. Everyone makes mistakes all the time. Not making the same mistake twice is the key.

Even the greatest master – the true expert – is only scratching the surface of the incredible complexity and subtlety in their garden. So scratch that surface yourself if only to find out how little you know. Back yourself. A lot of success in growing anything well is a blend of confidence and intuition. Have confidence in your intentions and build intuition by exercising it. Pay attention. Look carefully. Gradually, knowledge and intuition will combine to inform each other and make the next observation more meaningful. And so it continues.

It is easy to cast yourself in the role of a conductor, controlling every note and beat of the garden. But modesty is the only appropriate attitude. Even the best gardener is not so much a conductor as a cross between the caretaker making sure the light bulbs are replaced and the member of the audience with the best seat in the house.

Life is short and absurd and run through with pain and sorrow. But even in the face of real suffering, gardening can make our days shine with joy.

Gardens heal. When you are sad, a garden comforts. When you are humiliated or defeated, a garden consoles. When you are lonely, it offers companionship that is true and lasting. When you are weary, your garden will soothe and refresh you.

I have had a very fortunate life. I have made gardens with someone that I love and this has brought me great happiness. You need luck to be happy. But make a garden and you increase your chances.

I hope that this book helps make your garden.

The Seasons

Know and go with the seasons. Do not fight them – you will lose. This will not always be convenient, so learn to be flexible. And measure the seasons by your own backyard. When is it spring in your garden? How does winter lie there? At what point precisely is the shift from spring to summer? These are real questions and have precise answers that are different in every garden in the world. It is your autumn, your east wind, your shower of rain.

A good tip is to photograph your garden as much as possible and review the pictures out of season. It is a very useful way to map the seasons in your own garden. It is also an invaluable record of what was planted where and an aid to next year's planting plans. You will be astonished how memory plays false, both for good and ill.

Spring

Wait till your garden is buzzing before planting or sowing too much. After a long and dark northern winter, we all yearn for spring and celebrate every little sign – the first snowdrops, catkins, daffodils in the park, primroses flowering under a hedge – but the most critical indicator is the presence of bees and other pollinating insects. Two things happen in spring: the nights get shorter and the air – and critically the soil – gets warmer. The first process of lengthening days is inevitable and begins in mid-winter. But most spring plants do not really get going until warmth appears, too – not least because pollinators are few and far between in cold weather.

Traditionally farmers would go out into a field, drop their trousers and sit butt-naked on the ground to test the soil. This might raise an eyebrow or two down on the allotment, but the principle is sound. Wait until the soil is not cold to your touch before sowing any seeds outside. Ignore the date – plants do not read calendars – but pay great attention to the feel of the earth and trust your judgement.

March is the month of bulbs planted the previous autumn. Plan for that, enjoy them and do not force the pace. Be patient. Plants or seeds grown later in spring, when the soil and nights are warmer and the days longer, usually catch up and grow strongly and healthily.

Nothing in gardening is so exciting or encouraging as the lengthening days of April and May. Really take note of this increasing light and the way that it shines within the garden so you can plan for next year.

As a rule, spring flowers are best grouped and bunched together to make a localised but powerful hit. Most of the garden is still bare, so if you spread your spring flowers thinly, they can be overwhelmed by wintry emptiness. But if you make one area full of bulbs, hellebores, primroses, pulmonarias or any other early-flowering plants, then it sings out.

As a rule, spring flowers are best grouped and bunched together to make a localised but powerful hit

If you have very little space, pots planted with bulbs can be grouped together to provide that spring impact. As early as late January or in February, *Iris reticulata* varieties have intense colour, while snowdrops and 'Tête à Tête' daffodils all grow well in pots and can be induced to flower a little early to create a focussed display.

If you are not busy in the garden in spring, then you are probably wasting precious time. Yes, spring flowers were planted last autumn. But you can fill a whole long summer with a few weeks' work in spring.

You can get away with planting almost anything from snowdrops to hedges in early spring. Get it in the ground before the end of April, and it will grow and flourish. It is the time when you can do almost anything and at the very least get away with it.

Although there is a lot to do in the veg plot, pickings can be thin and it is for good reason that mid-April to mid-June was called the 'hungry gap'. Winter crops are finishing and summer ones yet to begin. It takes careful planning to get round this, with successional sowings of leaves like rocket and radish that grow quickly in cool weather as well as filling the ground ready for harvests later in summer.

Summer

Summer has two mini-seasons in most north European gardens. The first is a short but distinct period starting at the end of May, lasting no more than six weeks and finishing around the end of the first week of July. Throughout June the days are at their longest, the light at its brightest and all the deciduous foliage, be it of an aquilegia or an oak tree, is full but still fresh. Roses are at their best, large-flowered clematis are glorious and plants like irises, foxgloves, alliums and lupins crown the borders. There is a real sense of the garden coming magnificently into being but still rich with the promise of more to come.

But although June days can be hot, the nights can be surprisingly cold and these sharp variations are often more damaging to tender plants than the actual temperature itself. Plants from closer to the equator – tomatoes, pumpkins, dahlias, cannas – will react badly to this and their growth can slow right down, which is when they become prone to attack by predators.

Plants from the northern hemisphere, however, are responding to the long days, and as the nights get shorter – albeit hotter – they will start to set seed. In practice, this is when the second summer mini-season begins, and lasts well into September.

There is a gardening convention that August is a difficult month but that is not the case where I live. The Jewel Garden really hits its stride in August and September despite the shortening days, because the nights are warm. Dahlias, bananas, zinnias, tithonia, sunflowers, helianthus, nicotiana and cosmos are flowering exuberantly. This is when the falling light levels coupled with heat make the rich colours like plum, caramel, purple and ruby red glow richly.

The Jewel Garden in high summer »

12

Autumn

The year turns in on itself on 23 September, which is the autumn equinox. Day and night hang, too briefly, in balance, then tip towards the dark and the year is lost. Autumn can be beautiful. It can be rich with colour and smoky light, and it can be full of flower and fruit, but autumn is always sad. The party is over and the light all over the northern hemisphere is slipping away.

Autumn in Herefordshire smells fruity and alcoholic. A cidery tang floats through the air as thousands of orchards, many still made up of giant standard trees under-grazed with sheep, all hang heavy with their ripening fruit. My own garden with, in all, over 50 different varieties of apple, is dominated by them and although we gather a year's supply and carefully store them, the ground in the orchard lies strewn with falling fruit, which the dogs gorge on – with appalling digestive consequences.

It is not the chill in the evening air or the lashing autumn rain that carries the message of winter to plants and birds and – I am certain through my own experience – to humans, but the slightest change in day length. We can mollycoddle winter seedlings, using mulches, cloches, fleece and windbreaks to keep them cosy. But none of this is any good without enough light.

Whilst swallows fly south and humans repine, plants are more stoutly practical. Those such as roses, ash and apples have their winter hardiness increased by exposure to shorter hours of daylight, so any of them grown under artificial light, even with temperatures that exactly mirrored those in natural daylight, would be less hardy than identical plants grown under only the sun.

Despite the way that light, colour and human and plant energy are all on the wane, it is important to do as much as possible in autumn to set up the year ahead. As one door closes, another – rather smaller and more distant – opens. It is not so much a time to put the garden to bed as to gently prepare it for action.

This is when you should be planning for next summer, planting, moving and ordering plants. The more that you can get down between now and Christmas to prepare for spring, the better it will be for you and the garden. Of course, the great controlling factor is the weather but the beauty of this time of year is that most jobs can take place at any time over winter. If you have time, energy and enthusiasm, it is always best to make the most of the fading light.

Autumn leaves

There are not many Americanisms that I like but one which I love is the word 'fall' for autumn. In every way it perfectly suits the season, with its falling leaves. The degree of colour-change in fall is dependent upon late-summer weather, when hot days and cold nights stimulate the production of chemicals closely related to carbohydrates that produce red pigmentation. The leaves convert starch to sugar to feed the tree, but cold nights stop it moving from the leaf back to the roots. This accumulation of sugar in the leaves often results in red pigmentation and, as the green chlorophyll begins decomposing as the days shorten, so the red comes to the fore. The greater the difference in temperature between day and night – in other words the hotter the days between late July and early August – the more extreme the leaf coloration will be.

Yellow leaves are coloured by a different process. This is essentially the removal of chlorophyll – which produces green pigmentation – to reveal the yellow that is there all the time. The yellowest of all autumnal trees is the English elm, which you will only see in a juvenile version or in a hedgerow as, since 1975, all mature trees were killed off while young ones succumb to Dutch Elm disease at around 20ft or 15 years old. Incidentally, trees with yellow summer leaves will always be slower-growing than trees with green leaves as they are starved of the supply of sugars and starch that the chlorophyll helps deliver.

The leaves fall when cells break down in the layer between leaf stalk and twig. A corky scar forms over the wound that this causes, protecting the tree from infection. Some trees cannot form this scar tissue so they do not drop their dead leaves until the new ones are ready to push them off the following spring, which is why beech and hornbeam keep their russet leaves all winter. Poplar, birch and willow fall early but oak

can hang on well into December.

Evergreens do not change colour but very few hang on to their leaves for more than a year. In practice 'evergreen' means that the leaves can overwinter before being renewed in spring. However, although they do eventually fall to the ground, do not add evergreens to your leafmould pile as they take much longer to break down.

....

Leafmould

Leafmould is always useful and you can never have too much. It is low in nutrients but excellent for improving soil structure. This makes it very useful in homemade compost and as a mulch for woodland plants, as well as a general conditioner for a heavy soil.

For some reason, no one has ever commercialised it, although there is absolutely no reason why they should not do so – it is, after all, much easier to gather fallen leaves and make leafmould than rip up and destroy rare peat bogs to market the peat.

However, unlike good compost, which needs turning regularly and has to be made up of a good mixture of ingredients to get the right balance, leafmould is the easiest thing in the world to make. Garden compost is made by a mixture of bacterial, fungal, invertebrate and insect activity, stimulated by heat and oxygen, which is why you have to turn it. But leafmould is largely made by fungal activity and is 'cold', insofar as it does not need heat to spur the fungi into activity. You just gather deciduous leaves, make sure that they are thoroughly wet, put them to one side and let them quietly get on with the process of decomposition.

If the ground is dry enough, mowing up leaves is an excellent idea because it chops as it collects them and they have a greater surface area, which means they rot down faster as well as taking up much less space. In fact, I mow nearly all our leaves, very often depositing them on a long brick path in the garden, setting the blades of the mower high, and 'mowing' the path, gathering up all the leaves as I go.

« Every fallen leaf is gathered and stored in a chicken-wire cage to make leafmould

They then go into a large chicken-wire container so they have as large a surface area exposed as possible. Most years there is enough rain to keep them moist but in a dry year, I put the hose onto them every month. Either way, we invariably have perfect leafmould by the following October, when the container is emptied into bags. The resulting leafmould is used as mulch and also throughout the year as part of our potting mix. The wire bay container is then empty and ready for the new batch of leaves, to start the process all over again next autumn.

I appreciate that lots of gardens are not large enough to have a permanent large wire container for leaves. In this case, the answer is to put the leaves in a black bin bag, leaving the top turned but not tied. Make sure the leaves are really wet and punch a few holes in the bag to drain excess water. The leaves will rot down very well and can be stored behind a shed or tucked away in any corner for a year to quietly convert to a soft, powdery material that smells faintly of a woodland floor on a sunny autumnal afternoon.

Winter

Much as most humans might prefer winter warmth, our gardens are much healthier if they can have a few months of really sharp cold weather. Cultivated soil left in clods will break down and become lovely friable tilth simply through being frosted. Best of all, the dozens of fungal spores that afflict our warm, damp gardens are blitzed by sustained cold weather. Overwintering aphids and slugs and snails die off. A month of sustained cold in the garden does more to get rid of pests and diseases than a lorry load of chemicals could ever do.

And cold ground makes life much easier for the gardener. Mud becomes solid. You can walk dry-shod and push wheelbarrows full of muck or weeds over it.

There is, of course, a price to pay for this. The semi-tender plants that most of us grow in our borders, like salvias, penstemons, melianthus, jasmines, camellias and bay, will all suffer if the temperature falls much below −5°C. However, there are other plants

– from as diverse a range as garlic to primroses – that need a cold period in order to trigger their spring growth or germination.

Most temperate garden plants have adapted effective means to counter cold. Deciduous trees and shrubs drop their leaves and stop all but small root growth. Herbaceous plants will survive frozen ground perfectly happily because they have shut down all growth and gone into a state of hibernation. Annuals die as plants but leave a mass of seeds that will survive the cold and grow in spring. Biennials establish well enough to overwinter before growing fully the following spring.

Heavy snow is an excellent insulator, protecting plants beneath its blanket. It also is an important source of winter moisture if it thaws slowly enough to soak into the soil. But it can do a lot of damage to evergreens, especially topiary, and should be knocked off – after you have taken your pictures of them magically frothed in white.

Heavy snow is an excellent insulator, protecting plants beneath its blanket

Although extreme cold – below –12°C – will start to kill off a number of otherwise tough plants, cold on its own is not the biggest problem in winter. It is cold combined with wind and or wet that can turn a robust situation into horticultural disaster.

Wind chill can make all the difference to survival. Even a 20mph wind – officially classed as no more than a 'fresh breeze' – will turn freezing into –7°C, and –5°C into –13°C, which is into the red zone for many plants. Hedges, shrubs or even temporary netting that will filter the wind, can make a huge difference. In fact, the microclimate within a garden or even within different areas of a garden can vary greatly and mean otherwise quite tender plants survive harsh weather. This boils down to one word – shelter.

Evergreens are particularly vulnerable to damage from wind in winter because they are constantly transpiring and losing water. If there is a cold, dry wind, that water will not be replaced, and it is not uncommon for hardy plants, like box or holly, to have their leaves turn parched and brown, or even for the plant to die of winter drought, especially on roof gardens. This can happen very rapidly if the soil that they are in is frozen, as the roots will not be able to take up any water at all. One of the best solutions in very cold, dry weather is to spray the plants with water, which then freezes and forms a protective film around the leaves.

But there are times when the lack of wind is disastrous to the gardener for precisely the opposite reason. If your garden is on a slope with a building or wall at the bottom, cold air will flow down the hill, meet the wall and eddy back up – exactly like water. If your garden is at the bottom of a slope or in a natural basin, then it is important to let the wind in where you want it, flow through and get out again.

Hardy plants can manage down to extreme temperatures such as –15°C and can sustain cold of about –5°C for weeks or months. Half-hardy plants do not, as a rule, tolerate any temperatures below freezing but can withstand the general, lingering cold that characterises much of April or even May, while tender plants do not survive below –5°C.

Our long autumn and spring prepare plants for winter and summer alike. This is why sudden frost can have such disastrous effects – especially in spring. A plant that might withstand a month of bitter sub-zero temperatures can have half its growth killed by a few degrees of sudden frost in May. It sounds strange but, the longer and hotter the summer, the better trees and shrubs will be able to survive the cold of winter because their wood will have fully ripened.

Too rapid a thaw will kill a plant as effectively as too rapid a freeze. There must be time for the frozen water around the cells to slowly permeate back into them, otherwise the cells will be ruptured – hence the disaster caused by a really late frost, when the early-morning sun is hot and hits the frozen tissue before the air temperature has gradually risen and thawed it slowly.

Any protective layer is effective against light frosts, so cover or wrap tender or exposed shrubs, perennials and even vegetables in

The garden in winter »

horticultural fleece. Insulate the ground with newspaper, straw or a good layer of compost. This stops the surface roots freezing and is particularly important for evergreens. Wrap pots and statues in a protective layer to stop them cracking in frost.

....

Plants that survive cold especially well

Trees: Ash, beech, birch, black pine, ginko, hawthorn, holly, lime, maples, Norway spruce, oak, sorbus, *Thuja occidentalis*, willows

Shrubs: All Alba, Gallica and species roses (other than spring-flowering ones), *Buddleia davidii*, euonymus, heathers (acid soils only), *Kerria japonica*, mahonia, philadelphus, *Spiraea thunbergii*, many viburnums, winter jasmine

Herbaceous and perennial plants: Most true herbaceous plants including: bugle, *Echinops ritro*, *Iris sibirica*, *Geranium endressii*, *G. sanguineum*, hellebores, *Lamium maculatum*, primroses, *Pulmonaria saccharata*

Climbers: *Clematis viticella*, *Hydrangea petiolaris*, *Lonicera periclymenum*, *Wisteria floribunda*

Annuals and biennials: Agrostemma, cornflowers, nigella, Shirley poppies, sweet rocket

Bulbs: Crocuses, *Iris unguicularis*, *Lilium regale*, muscari, scilla, snowdrops, winter aconites

....

Birds in winter

The relationship between garden and birds changes when the leaves start dropping. For a start, the birds are more visible. They crowd the branches as a series of shapes. The outline of a small tree will suddenly break as a flurry of birds scatters, scared off from gobbling berries.

Winter bird sound is much harsher than in summer – a series of warnings rather than wooings. Occasionally a robin will astonish the afternoon with a burst of song, but November in my garden tends to shuffle with staccato sound, like overhearing an argument in another room.

Winter is heralded by the arrival of the fieldfares and redwings just as surely as summer is certified by the first swallow. But whereas the swallows, supple as mercury, arrive with a kind of soaring familiarity, the fieldfares are a curious mixture of truculence and shyness. Everything about them is harsh and jerky, yet I like them. They are of the season. They adore the apples left in the orchard best of all and will fiercely defend a tree surrounded by windfalls from other birds. They also do a lot of good, eating snails, leatherjackets and caterpillars.

The other winter thrush, the redwing, is smaller, daintier and altogether less intrusive. Whereas the fieldfare has an instantly recognisable grey/mauve head, the redwing is only really distinguishable from a song thrush when in flight, when the red flash under the wing is very visible – although its tendency to flock, like the fieldfare, is a giveaway.

Weather

We gardeners have to be on intimate terms with the weather. We deal with it all the time. We look up and read the sky, look around and measure what has happened and how it is playing out.

As far as the garden is concerned, weather is neither particularly good nor bad. It just is. Plants adapt and nearly always recover from a rough time. Most survive anything if they are planted in the right place.

The gardener cannot always get out and do the jobs exactly as planned but usually it really does not matter that much. Be flexible. Pay great attention to the weather and respect it but be patient. Bend to it rather than rail against it.

Rain has many horticultural meanings. Frost tells a story that may take weeks or even seasons to play out. Temperature is critical but subtle. Learning these stories is part of a good gardener's armoury.

The wind

Every wind comes brandishing a different weapon and every garden has its vulnerabilities depending on planting and aspect.

Get to know the wind. Sometimes it will be a fierce adversary and occasionally your friend, but it should always be familiar. Have a mind map of the wind in your garden and be aware of the implications of its direction.

In my garden, southerly winds are generally welcome because they quickly dry everything out – but it means we scurry round staking because they also buffet. Westerlies invariably bring rain and sometimes storms, northerlies carry snow, and the spring easterlies are devastating in their ability to cut like a blade of ice through everything – including the walls of the house.

Wind chill can turn an otherwise perfectly acceptable temperature into a lethal blast (see page 19). It can desiccate foliage and stress plants as well as misshape them. Be ready for this and create shelter where possible. If a planting is ailing, always check its exposure to wind even if plants around it seem fine.

Get to know the wind. Sometimes it will be a fierce adversary and occasionally your friend, but it should always be familiar

Gardeners also know – or should know – the detailed variations within their own backyards. Microclimates really matter within all but the tiniest garden. There are always bits of an otherwise seamless lawn that crunch underfoot with frost whilst the rest is still soft. Two identical plants within a yard of each other can fare completely differently because just one catches the wind that is funnelled through a gap in a hedge the other side of the garden.

Good weather for me is measured not by what I wear above the knees but by how I am shod. If I can walk round the garden without wellies, then it is a good day. But if I can garden carelessly, stepping from border to path to lawn with nary a second thought, wearing lightweight shoes, then the weather is perfect.

Nature

There is a traditional approach which assumes that gardening is some kind of battle to be won or lost. In this world view, the 'good' gardener is the one who triumphs over nature. This still exerts a strong force, aided and abetted by the purveyors of poisons and devices for killing as many creatures as possible in the garden. Whether it be slugs, ants, vine weevils, ground elder, couch grass, wasps, moles, greenfly, cold, mildew, drought, honey fungus – the list could go on – nature is out to ruin your domestic bliss. Only eternal vigilance and – of course – this snakeskin oil, so brightly and attractively packaged and so seductively advertised, can rescue you and your lovely garden from total disaster.

This is nonsense on every level. You need nature more than she needs you. It is not an equal relationship. Serve her well and she will look after you. Abuse her and everyone loses.

Every living thing – flora and fauna – on your land is accountable to you. That account must be paid. The books must balance so never take out more than you put in.

Doing no harm is usually more important than trying to do good. Often the best course of action is to do nothing whilst you watch and wait. Be modest in all things – including protecting the environment. It can usually get on just fine without your help.

Preserve the precious and rare. It is always the outliers – the rare, the small, the tenuous – that go first and when they go, they are very difficult to get back. What always survive are the most common and resilient. This means that species decline faster than individuals – in other words you end up with more of less. Diversity, not the number of plants or animals, is always the best measure of ecological health.

Cultivate insects. Regarding insects as 'bugs' or 'pests' is absurd. They are the most important visible wildlife in your garden. Value them accordingly. Create suitable habitats, provide food and never, ever, kill insects indiscriminately.

Revere fungi. Gardeners tend to regard all fungi as harmful. But do not be frightened of them. Only a tiny, tiny proportion do any harm at all and the vast majority are essential for life in the garden. Soil without fungi is barren. Fungal filaments can reach parts that even the tiniest roots cannot, and fungi form partnerships with all kinds of plants, from mosses to trees, taking elements from deep in the soil so plants can benefit from them and fungi can then feed on the sugars in the plants. Mushrooms and toadstools are the fruiting forms of fungi that then spread their spores.

Insects are the most important visible wildlife in your garden. Value them accordingly

We are ignorant and new knowledge is exposing how little we know. Discoveries are coming in that are astounding and revolutionary. For example, we now know that bacteria inside certain leaves are nitrogen fixing and that trees can take their nourishment from up to 11 miles away. Eleven miles! Have an open mind and do not cling to established knowledge or conventions.

The virtues of untidiness

Be untidy. Leave long grass, fallen leaves, rotting wood, patches of weeds, grass growing in the cracks, moss on the stone. These are all key habitats for important components of a healthy garden.

Always have some long grass growing. Nothing is more beneficial to insects than long grass. Ideally you have grass of varying lengths to provide a wide range of habitats, but a square yard of long grass will make all the difference.

Worms are as good a measure of soil structure and fertility as anything. There are over 25 species of earthworm in Britain and all play a huge role in tilling the soil. Their industry is staggering: worms move between 100 and 200 tons of soil a year per 2.5 acres, which is as much as any plough can do. Whether we appreciate it or not, the earth is literally moving beneath our feet.

There is still a general tendency to think of anything that 'disturbs' our soil, like earthworms, moles or ants, as pests that need controlling or eliminating. But these burrowers play an essential role in opening out the soil and incorporating organic material in it. So the next time a mole rearranges the architecture of your lawn, don't curse but be thankful for the work that it is doing for you.

Most so-called 'pests' are nearly always a symptom rather than the disease. Instead of trying to get rid of them, work out what you are doing to make them so welcome to your garden. Almost certainly you have upset the restraining, self-regulating balance. This is not – yet – a disaster. It can be regained – but not by isolating and zapping pests.

Cultivate bees. No bees, no garden, no humans. You do not have to keep bees yourself to attract them to your garden. Bees like flowers that are wide and open, and a range of these for as long a period as possible from spring through to autumn, will provide a steady supply of nectar for them.

Garden as you would be done by. The planet is not a remote concept but is right here. The Earth is your back garden. So do the right thing. Everybody wins.

Bumblebees love *Knautia macedonica* »

Place

Do not strive to make your garden like anywhere else on this earth. Copy, steal ideas, imitate and derive as much as you like, but only to create something that is unique and imbued with its own profound sense of place – otherwise you can end up going nowhere.

Imbue your plot with your life, your loves, your quirks and foibles. Make it uniquely your own.

Every garden must have its own personality, its own atmosphere and a real, tangible sense of not being anywhere else in the world. So always look to local materials – stone, wood, plants – first. Be true to the place.

We are ephemeral and make things that do not last. The place endures. It is the relationship – the tension – between these two that creates something interesting.

We bring nothing into this world and take nothing with us – but leave something of yourself in your garden. Make it personal. Garden your own story.

All gardens are made in layers, one on top of another, sometimes over many hundreds of years. They might be gossamer-thin or clumsily thick, but all build up over time like the layers of an onion. You are just another layer. It will remain, perhaps overlaid by many others, but it will act like roots, like organic matter in the soil. It will feed the soul of all the garden layers to come.

I would not want any garden of mine to be like anyone else's any more than I would not want my bedroom to be like a hotel room. I increasingly long for the personal and the idiosyncratic. I want as much as possible to be handmade, one-off and distinctive. I like gardens that have their own accent and their own rules, and are rich in dreams and memories that everyone can share but no one can replicate.

What private gardens have to offer that trumps any kind of public space, however sensitively designed, is the way in which the sense of place merges into the sense of self of the gardener. The boundaries disappear. You become garden and garden becomes you. That is the goal of all gardening, where plant and earth and human flesh flow easily one into another in an undramatic union, carried with all the nonchalant joy of birdsong or the rustle of evening leaves.

Every garden must have its own personality and a real sense of not being anywhere else. Be true to the place

Although a garden has a precise and geographical place, it can never be fixed in time. To try and fix it is doomed to failure. Turn your back and it is gone. We can and must plan and plant for a seasonal future or even years ahead, but time liberates every garden from the tyranny of perfection and precision. Time can promise and tempt and lead you astray, but the fleeting moment is always glimpsed from the corner of an eye. That is not its limitation, but its gift. Nothing to hold, nothing to measure, nothing to compete. Just here, now.

Design

Think long. Be patient. For three years, few will see what you are doing – it will all be in your mind's eye. Then the garden will reveal its true colours and after five years be looking like a youthful version of itself. At seven years, many will not be able to age it at all and by twelve years, everything save the trees will look mature. Thereafter you will be cutting back and constraining more than encouraging growth.

Only grow what you want to grow. There is a culture of selecting plants and then working out ways of growing or raising them. Turn this on its head. Find out what thrives on your plot and then make the very best that you can from this.

Do not try and be like anywhere else. Be like here. Elsewhere is interesting in its differences.

Do not be aspirational. Big is not better – just different. Scale alters every concept. So a garage for two cars is not the same as a multi-storey car park. Understand your scale and work with it.

By the same token, you can often take a big idea from a large garden and extract its essence so it sits easy in your small backyard.

The importance of beauty

Beauty is essential. It is never a trade-off. Make the most of all beauty and never sacrifice it at the altar of expediency. It is too high a price.

Add nothing ugly. Do not accept any existing ugliness as fixed. Remove and change it if possible, otherwise modify or screen it.

What we most carefully try and create in our gardens is always a good indication of what we lack. Hence the extraordinary lengths that Australians or Californians will go to in order to have a lush green lawn, or the protection some of us will give to tender plants that come from climates very different to our own.

Two plants are usually more interesting than one. How plants interact and complement each other is what makes a garden rather than a collection of botanical specimens.

Get to know every tiny idiosyncratic detail. Be aware of the light at every moment of the day and the season. Notice the shadows leaf by leaf. See how some sections of path always seem to be slippery. Notice how some plants, seemingly planted in full sun, cant and crane towards the light. Notice where the thrush sings as the light falls.

Do not accept any existing ugliness as fixed. Remove and change it if possible, otherwise modify or screen it

Make your garden a tactile place. Plant so you can let your hands touch, dabble and caress sensuous foliage as you pass. And allow different parts of the garden to have their moment in the spotlight and then, when done, retire to the wings for a while. Do not expect it all to do everything all the time. No garden can be performing all the time. Relish the different corners and sections as they come and go.

Water improves everything in a garden – sight, sound, scent, texture, light, range of plants, range of wildlife – and markedly improves the overall health of the whole mini ecosystem. It could be a small bowl, stream or a lake. They all work. But always add water.

Get your structure in early. A good and interesting garden can be created simply by planting hedges interspaced with grass. Then, when you are ready, you can lift the turf as and when you require to create your borders. But plan the structure carefully – moving a hedge is a tiresome business.

Plant hedges and trees when they are still very small. They will grow much faster and better for it, are much cheaper when small and will quickly catch up and overtake plants twice their size.

Do not fight lines of desire. Everybody will always take the most direct, easiest route even if it means stepping over the corner of a border or through a gap in a young hedge. Cater for this. Make utilitarian paths – to the compost heap, tool shed, greenhouse, front gate – straight, smooth and easy for barrows and muddy feet. But if you want to encourage a slower, more meandering route, then have curving paths and close off the sight line to where they are going – so you have to follow the set path to find out. Block off any possible short cuts (see page 40).

Grow grass. Mow it and call it a lawn. But do not try and make it 'perfect'. Life really is too short. Smooth and green and smelling of new-mown grass when cut is good enough for me.

Let your garden be charming. This is such an important aspect of a good garden. Only you can be the judge of this, so look for and relish its charm.

Sit in the sun. Choose your places to sit where the sun falls at sitting times of day. If your garden is big enough, have a seat for all suitable sitting occasions – a cup of coffee before going to work, relaxing in the midday sun, enjoying the last lovely light of evening. Just a perch will do, even if it is in the middle of a border.

Make somewhere private. You cannot properly relax in your own garden if you feel overlooked or watched. It might only be big enough for a single seat but create somewhere that is truly private where you can go and metaphorically close the garden door behind you. It will transform your sense of ownership and possession.

Divisions and dimensions

The smaller the space the more you should fill it. Make borders wide and paths narrow. It is a common mistake to make a thin strip of border around the edge of a small garden as it only makes everything look meaner and pinched.

Most small gardens can even be divided up. A long, thin garden can be divided at least once by a wall, hedge or fence accompanied by just a narrow path and perhaps a gate. It will immediately make the garden seem bigger, add range and diversity, and create smaller spaces that are more human. But this rule can be broken with spectacular success.

The brick path in the Writing Garden was originally the floor of an outhouse »

The basic point of reference in a garden is the human body. You should always refer back to this. So 6ft is a good height for a dividing hedge; an arm's stretch – 4ft – is good for a low hedge; a pace – 3ft – is right for a narrow path; and a pace and a half – 5ft – is the width of two people walking comfortably side by side.

Watch the sun rise and set as often as possible. Shape the garden to capture this – cut gaps in hedges, prune branches. Let the sun in.

Neaten the verticals. The eye always runs to the edge of things. Keep these edges straight and neat – entrances, exits, edges, openings – and the unruliness contained by them is enhanced, modified and forgiven.

Very few gardens are big enough to hold half the plants we would like to grow and most of us have to dramatically limit our range

Play to your strengths. We all have the desire to do what we are not good at, to enlarge and expand our range and our idea of ourselves. But there is probably a good reason why you and your garden are not successful at something or other. So keep it simple. Do what you do easily and do it well.

Very few gardens are big enough to hold half the plants we would like to grow and most of us have to dramatically limit our range and choice of plants and planting styles simply through lack of space. Make a virtue of this. Edit hard (see page 49) so everything in your garden feels essential.

I love the way that even the tiniest garden can be loaded with all the aspirations of its maker and be perhaps flawed, scruffy or odd, but above all individual. When I fly over the suburban landscape coming into land back in the UK, or zoom through a built-up area in a train, I do not see row after row of identical streets but thousands of back gardens, all lined side by side and all triumphantly different. If that means accepting mess and disorder and 'bad' gardening, then three cheers for these things.

A sense of place

A 'good' garden, above all should have a sense of place. In order to come alive, it must above all, be profoundly there. By this I mean that every garden must have its own personality, its own atmosphere and a real, tangible sense of not being anywhere else in the world.

I have often heard people attempt to praise a garden by likening it to another more famous or grander one, but I regard that as failure. The best and most enjoyable gardens are often allotment plots — higgledy-piggledy and cheek by jowl, often in unremarkable municipal corners, all rented and effectively borrowed for a short growing season, and yet every plot claimed and cared for and loved – precisely because they are so personal and direct.

The transience of gardens

Gardens are above all places of flux. The changes are the thing itself, not the spaces between events. Some of that is inevitable and uncontrollable through the agents of seasons, weather and growth. But as a gardener I want to be part of that flow rather than trying to arrest it and pin it down like someone scrambling around trying to lay out pieces of paper in a breeze.

I want my gardens to be transient, dancing and always just out of my control rather than pinned to the page. However, as any good gardener knows, nothing is so hard as to give the appearance of doing nothing whilst still retaining the spirit and essence of what you want from your garden.

You have to give gardens licence to change – and the chances are that this will not happen as you planned or even wanted. It becomes – if you get it right – something more than an extension of your own costive art and craft.

There is a temptation to do what you think you ought to do or what you think others might enjoy. But gardens have to come from the heart or else they will never reach the head. You have to please yourself first and foremost or else you run the risk of pleasing nobody.

Some people would start this process by working on a planting list,

refining it as they went with a plantsman's sophistication. But to my mind, individual plants no more make a border or garden than individual colours make a painting. It is what you do with them and how they relate to each other that matters most. Yes, you choose your palette, which in turn is dictated by those plants that you know will thrive in any given situation, but that is only the beginning of an almost permanent editing process.

In other words, having prepared the site, decided what to plant, gathered the plants together and chosen where to plant them, dug holes and put them in the ground, nothing is finished. The game is just beginning.

« The garden in winter seen from the top of the house

Walking and Sitting

There are two types of garden path. One type is purely functional to take you quickly from A to B on a dry, firm surface. This is ideal to go to the shed or compost heap. These paths invariably follow 'lines of desire' (see page 33) so make the path simple and straight in the first place or make it impossible to deviate from it by blocking the way.

The second type of path exists to lead you where you can best appreciate the garden through which it passes. This might be a path that meanders through a border, a very wide path to encourage chat and slow walking or a narrow one to speed things up. It might be of old bricks laid on end that has a cottagey feel or chipped bark for a wildlife area or York paving slabs in a formal garden. In other words, the surface and design of the path will strongly influence how you use it and how you feel about the surroundings. Being aware of all the options and effects they have will help you make the best choices.

Finally, a path should always arrive at something or somewhere. Create focal points with containers or plants that make you want to follow the path to them.

Sitting

Every garden should have somewhere dedicated to sitting, preferably with a table so you can also eat outside. Often the best place for it is at the back of the house – but it is not the only option. In fact, the key to working out the best place to create a seating area in any garden is to ask yourself when and how you are going to use it.

The rule is to follow the sun. If you rarely sit out in the morning, then establish where the sun falls in the evenings between April and October and make your seating area there – even if that means doing so at the far end of the garden. If it is important to you to have an early morning cuppa sitting in the garden, then map out the morning sunshine. The moral of the story is always work with the unchangeable conditions and make the most of them, rather than blindly follow convention.

Every garden should have somewhere dedicated to sitting, preferably with a table so you can also eat outside

Although most gardens only have room for one main patio or permanent seating area, make sure that there are places to sit and enjoy the sun throughout the day – even if it is just a single seat or log set in amongst a border or against a fence.

Colour

So often you hear people refer to a 'riot of colour' as though that was intrinsically a good thing but in truth, a riot quickly becomes wearying if not downright dangerous.

Colours in the garden are there to be selected and managed as carefully as in any painting or wardrobe. Some work well together, others do not. Some appeal to you, others never feel right however much another may love them. The key is to choose your colours and choose them well.

Don't let yourself be accountable to the taste police. If you like a colour – any colour – then luxuriate in it. I like orange flowers and would be very sorry not to have tithonias, leonotis, heleniums, eschscholzias, zinnias, marigolds, orange dahlias and cannas, or the orange *Buddleia globosa*. But I have a good friend who cannot countenance the thought of a single orange flower in her garden. Each to their colourful own. There is never a right or wrong in these things. Just what feels most right for you and your garden.

Combine colour carefully. Don't just chuck it all at a border thinking that the more colour you plant, the more colourful the result will be. Just like a painter's palette, too much colour quickly muddies. Choose a colour theme, keep it simple and stick to it.

Opposites intensify and similar shades dilute and add complexity; use both to create the effect you want. So a brilliant blue iris or a purple clematis will become even more intensely blue or purple if orange tithonia is planted next to it. Likewise, the colours of a collection of old-fashioned roses in various ruffles and flounces of pink, set perhaps amongst mauve *Verbena bonariensis* or lavender, can have the effect of adding depth and complexity to each other without diminishing the overall effect.

The Jewel Garden »

Light and colour

Choose your colours to match the light. The light at different times of day and year affects how we see and react to colour more than any other factor. Use this. So rich plums, burgundies and oranges look better in evening light and best of all in late summer and early autumn, when the mix of light and direction maximises their velvet intensity. Pastels, on the other hand, look best in the much clearer morning light. White is lost in midday sun but looks fantastic at dusk.

Under a Mediterranean winter sky, pale, bleached-out greys, blues and sandy shades look subtle and rich with texture. The light is thin but bright and clear. However, in a British winter, you need as much dark green as possible to counter the gloom of brown and grey that dominates once all deciduous leaves have fallen. Use green to create structure, with evergreen hedges and topiary, and you have a winter garden – stark, strong but rich with colour.

Likewise, the soft morning light of a May or June day in Britain is perfect for pinks, primrose yellows and pale blues that glow and shimmer. These would be washed out and lost a thousand miles further south. Similarly, the intense blues, chrome yellows and oranges that look so dramatic in a Spanish or Moroccan garden under the midday sun become lifeless under northern cloud. It all comes back to working with nature – including the natural light.

In my garden we have used colours to define the planting in various areas of the garden. The most dramatic is the Jewel Garden. This uses ruby reds, amethyst purples, sapphire and lapis blues and emerald greens of all shades as the core colours, with gold, silver, brass and bronze touched with the bright oranges of topaz and citrine, and plenty of burgundies and plum colours.

The effect is rich, dramatic and lustrous. But it is rarely subtle, is rather late coming into its own in spring and is at its best in low evening light. It works wonderfully well as a vibrant centrepiece but might be a bit overpowering as the sole colour palette of the garden.

Colours are affected as much by what you do not use as those you select. For example, in the Jewel Garden we have absolutely no white nor any shade of pink other than magenta (a pink so blue that it is almost purple). The Mound has no red at all yet the Writing Garden – officially all white – has touches of pink and pale yellow in spring because it is surrounded by fruit trees smothered in pink blossom and underplanted with thousands of daffodils. Everything needs context.

....

Green and other colours

You can never have too much green. Every garden should be set amongst lots and lots of green. All other colours then work from this base. A white garden is in fact a green garden with white highlights. Rich, jewel colours glow from an equally rich palette of greens. Green is endless in its variations and is the colour that begins and ends all planting. A garden that is just green can be – and usually is – a beautifully calm and inspiring place.

You can never have too much green

Pink is the hardest colour to get right but it is worth the attempt. When it works in harmony with all the tones around it, neither too aggressively red nor ominously blue, not sickly sweet and not washed out, it creates a mood of buoyant celebration like no other floral colour. Pink works well with pink, with many shades of green, and with pale blues and white. But pale pinks amongst rich colours are mutually toxic.

You have to experiment and allow yourself to make mistakes. When we started planting the Jewel Garden we used white to represent diamond and silver. But it did not work. White is both an absence of colour and a moderator of the colours around it. So we removed all the white plants and now use glaucous blue from the foliage of plants such as cardoons to provide the suggestion of silver.

Colours set the emotional mood as much as any other factor. Walking in the Jewel Garden in high summer is like plugging into the mains, charging and recharging all aesthetic batteries with direct energy through the combination of all those rich jewel colours.

But just a few yards away – separated by the cool green corridor of the Long Walk – the Cottage Garden positively wallows in pastel tones.

Mauve, lilac, lemon, pinks of every hue and soft blues combine in an easy jumble of soft shades. This inevitably means that it is a gentle place, short on drama and energy but long on peace and relaxation. Colour has painted the mood.

The Writing Garden is notionally a white garden. But such a thing is at best a compromise and at worst garishly devoid of any colour at all. It is terribly easy to overdo white in any border but especially if the pristine, cool purity of a white garden is your intention. The secret is to have just enough white amongst masses of green of many different shades, and no more. The white flowers should ride the waves of green like the surf rather than swamp it like snowfall.

Marginal colours

Some colours are always marginal. Black – such as *Ophiopogon planiscapus* 'Nigrescens' – is fun but tricky, whilst the black silhouette of bare branches against a winter sky has a stark, gaunt beauty. Orange can be very right with other 'hot' colours but also glaringly wrong. And some yellows just don't seem to work with anything.

Magenta is interesting. A plant like the perennial *Geranium* 'Anne Folkard', with its lemon-green foliage and magenta flowers that run almost like a climber through neighbouring plants, is brilliant in our Jewel Garden for adding energy to almost everything around it. But in amongst pink roses, it seems crass and crude. Try things. Sooner or later you find what colours work as and when you want them to in your garden.

The colour of hard surfaces really matters, too. Treat them with the same care as you would any flower in a border. Keep them subtle and muted but where possible, also warm. It is the colour as much as anything else that makes York or Cotswold stone so alluring. Fences can and often should be painted but are best acting as a backdrop rather than a coloured feature in their own right. Shades of grey, green and pink can work well but blue is usually aggressively dominant.

« *Ammi majus* has the perfect delicate balance of white and green

A New Plot

Before you can begin to plan what you want your garden to become, you must first take stock of what it is.

There are a number of stages to this. The first is just go and have a good look. It is extraordinary how quickly we stop looking properly at what is familiar. You must sort the wheat from the chaff and analyse carefully what you wish to keep and what you want to reject. So go out into your garden and consciously look at it as though it was the first time you have ever laid eyes upon it.

Then take lots of pictures of it from every aspect. A camera often shows you things that your brain glides over or focuses too hard upon.

Plan to remove everything that you are sure you do not want. Never give anything the benefit of the doubt. You do not have to include anything just because it is there. At this stage, the right plant in the wrong place is wrong.

Measure your garden (you can simply pace it) and draw an accurate scale plan of the site, marking in everything that is there. This can be daunting but I strongly urge you to try because even the process of doing it is very revealing. Inevitably things will be spaced in ways that surprise you. I guarantee there will be much more or less space in some areas than you have been taking for granted, or the garden may actually be much longer and narrower or more rectangular than you have assumed. Only mapping it out on paper will reveal this.

When you have an accurate scale plan of your garden as it is now – even if it is apparently 'empty' of all but an old shed, a couple of scruffy shrubs and some bad lawn – then you can start to plot in your ideas and dreams. It is a good idea to use tracing paper for this stage so that the original plan remains unmarked and is always there to refer to. This also means you can have many different tracing-paper versions until you are satisfied that you have got it exactly right.

Once you are happy with what is on paper, you can then transfer the plan onto the ground using canes and thick white string. When you have done this, look at it from an upstairs window and live with it for a few days. The chances are that what seemed a good idea on paper does not quite transfer onto the ground. Paths might need widening or curves and angles adjusting. Make the changes then look again. Take your time. It is much easier to rectify mistakes at this stage than it is later on.

See what works locally

See what is growing well in your neighbourhood – it will not be happening by chance. If there are pines, rhododendrons, camellias and heathers, then you will have acidic soil and anything alkaline-loving, like lavender, rosemary, lilac or yew, will have a hard time of it. However, if there are lots of spring-flowering shrubs like ceanothus, clematis, lavender and philadelphus, then you will not be able to grow ericaceous-loving plants so easily.

You need to be realistic about your soil, aspect and climate. The type of garden you have will inevitably be influenced, in the future if not immediately, by the place where you live, and unless your garden is working with the natural environment, it will not thrive. Plants that need warm conditions will not grow well in an icy, blasted site. Others that need lots of moisture cannot be expected to last in an area with very low rainfall and free-draining soil.

This does not mean that you cannot create artificial environments like a pond or a scree garden, but in general it is best to choose the plants that thrive in your immediate neighbourhood.

Edit, edit and edit again

Many gardens fail because they try and do too much rather than too little. Decide on the one thing that you most want from your garden and make it the central, dominant element, even if that means excluding other desirable aspects.

There has to be some compromise and a lot of editing. The secret is

to keep the heart of the garden strong and clear, and dispense with all the peripherals.

So if you want a cottage-style garden, then create large borders packed with a gentle medley of pastel-coloured flowers, along with herbs, fruit and perhaps some vegetables.

If you want a formal, elegant garden, keep it symmetrical, balanced and very simple. Avoid clutter and clashing colours.

But remember that a garden is whatever you want it to be. Challenge some of the preconceptions of a 'good' garden. Do you really want a lawn? If you have children, then it is almost certainly a good idea but in a small garden, a lawn is hard to look after and keep looking good. Its function as an open space can often be better performed by a paved area, which will have the advantage of being a firm, dry surface all year round.

Similarly, you do not have to have flowers. I have seen stunning gardens that are entirely green.

Do not be frightened of being generous with scale. Most flower borders are too small. Make them as big as possible. A few large plants make a space seem bigger, whereas lots of small ones will make it feel crowded.

Divide and rule

Whilst it is important to keep gardens structurally simple and the layout uncluttered, few gardens cannot be subdivided. In many cases, using an obvious device such as a wall, hedge or fence (see page 34) will work perfectly satisfactorily.

However, the subdivisions can be more subtle. A group of pots that you have to walk around can take you into an area of specialised planting either of type or colour. Strategically positioned grasses or shrubs can signpost a change of tone or rhythm. Creating a change of level with steps rather than just following the slope will also create a new space and the potential for a change of planting.

« Looking through from the Walled Garden to the courtyard
and steps beyond

However you do it, think of the garden as a series of interlinked spaces rather than as one complete, integral canvas. The best analogy is with a house. Although it can work to spectacular effect, few people choose to eat, sleep, wash, cook and relax in just one vast room. So it is with any garden. Break it down into its component parts.

Add height

Do not be shy of adding height. Small trees such as crabs, maples and cherries, tall herbaceous plants and grasses that can be cut back hard in winter or spring, freestanding columns covered in climbers, a pergola or summer house – all can work well, even in limited spaces.

Money spent on strong, high fences is a good investment and will provide as much opportunity for a floral display as the borders – as well as providing privacy and protection. The barriers do not have to be impenetrable. Trellis above a solid fence provides support and filters the wind as well as leaving some connection with your neighbours.

Plan for all seasons

When we think of our dream garden it is usually high summer and perfect weather. That day will come but the brutal truth is that there will be many more days of cloud, wind and rain, and limited growth.

The key to having a garden that still looks good on the dankest winter's day is to provide good structure using hard landscaping and clipped evergreen plants. This could include topiary, low hedges or just the silhouette of bare branches. How you do it will depend upon your chosen style of garden, but always plan from the outset for winter as well as for your favourite flower-filled season.

It also means making sure that certain plants are holding your attention when little else is performing. Early-flowering spring shrubs and trees, shrubs and climbers with superb autumn foliage, shrubs with bright bark, containers filled with bulbs that flower in the first few months of the year, plants that age and weather well like grasses – all these will extend the seasons.

Prepare the soil

Time spent on preparing the soil is never wasted. Dig any areas that are to be planted – including proposed lawn areas – digging them at least a full spade's depth and breaking the soil up. They can then have compost or well-rotted manure spread over them and worked lightly into the soil; your garden will grow twice as well as a result.

The garden of any new house is bound to have compacted soil as a result of machines being used whilst it was being built. This compaction is usually covered over with a thin layer of topsoil and/or turf but will never go away and will stop almost all plants growing at all well.

If you are unable or unwilling to dig for any reason, then at the very least, add a thick layer of good garden compost or well-rotted manure to enrich the soil and improve its structure.

A new plot at a glance

1. **See** what is growing well in your neighbours' gardens as a guide to what will thrive in yours.
2. **Take** careful stock of what you have, including establishing the points of the compass, and plot it on an accurate scale plan of your garden. Use a scale of 1:50 or 1:100. Trace all your ideas over this.
3. **Plan** for the whole year, not just for high summer.
4. **Use** the whole garden, including all the vertical surfaces.
5. **Divide** and rule – break the plot up into separate spaces.
6. **Paths** should always take you somewhere different: give them a focal point.
7. **Plan** the garden around the best areas for sitting in rather than automatically putting your seating outside the back door.
8. **Make** big borders.
9. **Keep** it simple and edit ruthlessly.

The Small Town Garden

Most people live in towns and suburbs where space is at a premium, therefore most people have a small garden, and with the population steadily increasing, gardens are likely to go on getting smaller. So it has been pointed out to me – not always kindly – that my own garden is too large to have relevance to an 'ordinary' garden.

But there is no hierarchy of horticultural pleasure. The smallest garden can be as rewarding and meaningful as the largest. A small garden is doubly precious precisely because it is small, so everything in it is treasured and noticed daily. Also, small gardens can, with careful planning and plant selection, be extraordinarily powerful and fulfilling, whatever their style or the expectations you have from them. I know of plenty of rather empty, large gardens and tiny ones that are fascinating and deeply satisfying to be in.

What to leave out

The first and most important decision when making the small garden of your dreams is knowing what to leave out. Small spaces can never do everything. The danger is that if you attempt to cram too many different ideas, plants or functions into a small garden, the whole thing becomes a mishmash.

Keep it simple. By far the most successful small gardens do one thing very well. If sitting outside reading a book in the garden is your idea of heaven, then base the whole design around that dream. If you wish to eat and entertain outside, then make the seating area big enough for a table and work around that. If you collect plants of a certain type, then make the garden ideal for them. If your children need somewhere to play, then you are going to have to compromise on

Hostas, shuttlecock ferns and primulas thrive in shade »

precious plants. And so it goes. It means being clear, making decisions and sticking to them.

This applies to borders as well. Work out the effect you are trying to achieve, be it a riot of herbaceous perennials, the cool sensuality of grasses or a working veg patch, and focus on that. It is also easier and less stressful to look after because everything can be geared in one direction.

This is not to say that you cannot have variety and surprise. In fact, not to do so would be boring. But the variety and surprises should work around your core theme or idea rather than compete with it.

A small garden is best working towards a lot of seasonal changes that follow in sequence rather than changes occurring in parallel. So plant for all four dimensions: height, breadth, depth – and time. Use bulbs, annuals, climbers with good foliage as well as flowers – anything to extend the temporal range of display within the garden and thus maximise the potential of the limited space.

Go with the flow

Grow what wants to grow. Choose the plants that will thrive in your immediate neighbourhood (see page 49).

So if your garden gets very little light and is in shade for most of the day, make a virtue of that and specialise in plants that delight in shade. Ferns, ivy, mahonias, tiarellas, cyclamen, hostas, hardy geraniums and sweet woodruff are just a few that thrive in the relative dark and which can look superb.

Secondly, prepare the soil well. The great luxury of a small space is that this does not take long even if it involves a major effort. Many new gardens are horribly compacted with a thin layer of topsoil covering a multitude of construction-site sins (see page 53). Prepare the borders properly, get rid of the rubble and compaction, and add lots of organic goodness. You are asking a lot out of your limited space so you have to put a lot in.

Unless you want a play area for children, lawns are not usually a good idea in a very small garden. The effort of cutting them does not justify a lawn mower and a scruffy patch of grass will always be just that – scruffy.

The most common mistake that I come across in a small back garden is to have a lawn occupying most of the area with just a ribbon of soil a foot or so wide at the base of the fence. This has the effect of emphasising the lack of space. If you want a lawn, consider having a path between borders that takes you to it as a separate space, or having a circular lawn ringed by generous planting that creates an illusion of more space than there is.

Instead of a lawn, it might be better to have a hard landscaped area with exactly the right surface you want – paving, bricks, cobbles, slabs, or whatever you like. A paved area is also much more useful for a sitting area and much less work. And it makes the ideal place for pots.

But you do not need to have an open space at all. The entire garden can be filled with plants, with only a narrow path providing access and a small space just big enough for a couple of seats and a small table, so that you sit surrounded by colour and fragrance. The only rules to follow are the ones that matter to you.

Pots

A small garden will take both a large number of small pots packed together as well as a few very large ones. Any outsized object or plant can look perfectly at home in a tiny space as long as you are ruthlessly selective about it. If it does not look absolutely right, then get rid of it. Every single thing should delight you. There is literally no room for compromise. You must ask yourself about every individual plant, every paving stone, each pot, whether it is the best use of that particular space, whether it is the right thing in the wrong place.

Most of us make decisions about what materials we use as a result of practical limitations rather than absolute choice. We have limited money, time and energy and do the best with what we can get. But the smaller the garden, the less that works.

Be painstaking and patient. It is better to use nothing and wait, than use the wrong thing. Aim to get it right all the time and be prepared to constantly alter things in the quest for perfection. This attention to detail is the heart and soul of looking after a small space.

....

Division

No garden is so small that it cannot be divided into smaller spaces. A long thin town garden can be made into two or even three smaller square or rectangular spaces joined by a path. A square patio garden could have two levels. An empty rectangular garden could have one area that is open and coolly controlled leading to another that is heavily planted and intense – or vice versa. This is not say that it should be, just that you should consider the advantages of breaking your small town garden into separate areas.

No garden is so small that it cannot be divided into smaller spaces

The division could be made with a solid brick wall or with an evergreen hedge like box or yew – semi-solid deciduous hedges that are ideal for filtering the wind and are transparent in winter – or even with a low hedge you can see over but have to walk round, or with trellis that you can see through. Any kind of division will invite you on and in, and also create the opportunity for varied planting or colours.

Of course, each little bit of the garden has to harmonise with the whole. It cannot be assembled like a patchwork quilt but if one area does not work or is spoilt by one bit of bad planting, the whole garden is not ruined. This approach has its drawbacks though – it involves more work than a more unified plan and can get fiddly. But the beauty of a small garden is that it responds wonderfully to time put into it.

....

Be generous!

One of the most common mistakes people make when designing a small space is to think that everything in it must be small. The opposite is usually true. A few large plants make a space seem bigger whereas lots of small ones make it feel crowded. There are many small trees such as crab apples, maples and cherries that the smallest garden will accommodate, and every garden can include height, especially with tall herbaceous plants and grasses that can be cut back hard in winter or spring so they do not become overly dominant.

Use every tiny space for planting. The gaps in walls are ideal for herbs like thyme, flowers like *Aubrieta deltoidea* and the tiny daisy *Erigeron kravinskianus*, while the cracks in paving are perfect for the creeping mint *Mentha requienii*, *Alchemilla mollis* and the rock rose *Helianthemum nummularium* amongst others.

Climbers

Walls and fences are the same height in a tiny garden as a large one so their vertical importance increases as the horizontal area decreases. Every inch of wall or fence should be used. This also makes for many more opportunities for some privacy – even if it is only a solitary seat – which I regard as essential if you are to fully relax in your garden.

Plant all your climbers at least half a yard from the fence or wall. They will grow much better for it. But plant them close together, every yard or so. You can get away with the inevitable overlap by mixing their flowering seasons. So a *Clematis alpina* can grow through a climbing rose with perhaps a *C. viticella* taking over in August.

Use ivy and *Hydrangea petiolaris* alongside a rose like *Rosa* 'Souvenir du Docteur Jamain' on a shady wall. Mix and mingle them to create the green, soft barrier you need together with colour and scent. I would also invest in really strong trellis to support them.

Within the garden, wigwams can support annual climbers like sweet peas, the cup and saucer vine, morning glory or the Chilean glory flower. These will all grow in a container, too.

Late-flowering clematis like *Clematis viticella* can sprawl through shrubs or trellis and be cut hard back every year so they do not overspill their space. Small gardens are often very sheltered, so gloriously scented jasmine, *Trachelospermum jasminoides* and *Clematis armandii* can thrive, whereas they might be too exposed in a large garden.

The perfect small garden tree

In a small garden, a tree is going to have to work hard to justify its space and must therefore be chosen carefully. The Japanese maple, *Acer palmatum*, fits the bill admirably, making it the ideal small garden tree, with its low mounds of finely cut leaves glowing with autumn colour. It is as happy in a container as in the ground and, as long as it is sheltered from drying winds and has reasonably moist air, is easy to grow. It does not like chalk or limestone but a good rich neutral to acid soil with good drainage suits it perfectly. *A. p.* 'Atropurpureum' will eventually reach some 20ft in height and the finely cut leaves of *A. p.* var. *dissectum* add a level of finesse to what is already a highly sophisticated tree. It is no wonder that the Japanese revere it.

Maples are not prone to any special problems although the leaves can be damaged by aphids, which will make them misshapen. But the biggest problem with any maple is wind scorch. This is especially true if you live by the coast and have salt-laden winds. Grow your maples in a sheltered spot, away from the morning sun so they avoid sun scorch on frosty days and above all are protected from cold, drying winds.

Water

Quite a small amount of water movement can transform an entire garden, adding music, energy and sparkling light, as well providing the setting for a whole range of planting. A dark wall can host a simple cascade made from a spout running down the wall into a basin from which the water is pumped a few feet back up and round again. This then is the ideal environment for shade- and moisture-loving ferns and transforms a difficult area into a really attractive feature.

If you want to be more ambitious, it is perfectly possible to make a stream, complete with pools, rocks and little cascades. All you need is a fall in level from the top to bottom. This can be created in a level site by putting the spoil from the pond at the bottom of the stream at the top of the run and then landscaping the fall/stream with stones and cobbles to make it look natural. The stream can curve and wind through borders or natural contours, or run straight like a canal.

The principle is exactly the same as it is for the wildlife pond, using a waterproof liner (see page 89) along the length of the stream with the edges covered by soil and stones. Stones placed in the stream will break the flow and will add texture to the sound as the water gurgles past them.

On the other hand, the very simplest moving water feature is still wonderfully satisfying. A bubble of water rising up through a container of pebbles breaks and washes back over and through them into a small reservoir below, and back up again. A simple terracotta urn, filled with water, could have a central fountain that just breaks the surface and then overflows down into a reservoir. The urn sits on supports above a sunken reservoir and a rigid pipe for the water is fed through a hole in the bottom of the urn.

The Japanese, who mastered the art of making exquisite small gardens more than any other culture, have perfected the delightful *Shishi-odoshi* or deer scarer. A length of bamboo is hinged horizontally through another, larger vertical section that conceals a pipe bringing water up from a hidden tank. This water spills from another, smaller, bamboo spout onto the hinged wood. The weight of the falling water forces the hinged piece of bamboo down and, as it descends, the water runs out and it flips back under its own weight, banging against a strategically placed stone as it does so and with the bamboo making a musical 'clack'. Depending on the rate of flow – which is easy to adjust, this can be made to happen at a desired interval.

Whatever you decide to make in your garden, the secret is to harness the musical element that always accompanies running water. It is not only stimulating but also deeply restful.

These small but very effective water features are best planted simply, using predominantly green to reinforce the cool, sensual feel of the moving water. Bright colours distract and diminish the impact.

I love the combination of shade, water and ferns. These are a few ferns that work well.

Dryopteris filix-mas has elegantly arched fronds and loves shade, although it will adapt to moist or dry conditions.

The aspleniums, or spleenworts, with their seaweed-like flat fronds, come in many different sizes, from the tiny *Asplenium trichomanes* to the dramatic *A. scolopendrum* (Crispum Group). They are superb plants for damp shade and will grow in the cracks in stone and brick.

The athyriums, or lady ferns, such as the native *Athyrium filix-femina* and cultivars, need some moisture in the soil.

The shuttlecock fern, *Matteuccia struthiopteris*, is dramatic but easy once established, dying down to a brown knobbly stump in winter from which sprout yard-high fronds in spring.

Maidenhair ferns such as *Adiantum venustum* with its delicate, shimmering fronds, make superb groundcover.

Blechnum spicant, the hard fern, and the oak fern, *Gymnocarpium dryopteris*, both relish the shady, damp air of a fountain.

The small town garden at a glance

1. **Be** quite clear what you want from your garden. Small gardens rarely do more than one thing well but that can be enough to make a beautiful, completely pleasing space.
2. **Keep** it simple and avoid clutter. If you want lots of different plants, then have large beds and accept that there will be room for little else. Otherwise focus on a core of plants and a planting style, and allow these to come through strongly.
3. **Get** it right. The smaller the garden, the less room there is for compromise. This does not necessarily mean spending more money but usually means spending a bit more time sourcing exactly what you want.
4. **Always** start with a seating area and having established the best

'Madame Alfred Carrière' growing on the west wall of
the Walled Garden »

spot in the garden for this, work everything else around it. It does not have to be near the house but it does have to feel relaxed, sunny and slightly private.

5. **Use** as many vertical surfaces as possible, both for climbers and within a border. The smallest garden has much the same opportunities for growing upwards as the largest.

6. **A** small garden should be over-planted initially and then thinned as plants grow. Otherwise you have a few years of bare soil.

7. **Do** not fall into the trap of lots of little things. Big plants, containers and materials make a small space seem bigger.

8. **We** can take inspiration from any garden, of any shape or size, and apply it to our own. It might just be a plant combination or the way some steps are made or a climber trained. But there is always something to be learned, however small your own garden.

The Cottage Garden

Cottage gardens are filled with charm, innocence and a sense of harmonious abandonment. Blowsy, soft, and overspilling with colour and scent, they can and do look superb in any location, urban or rural. No other style of garden works so well to create a flower-filled retreat from the hard edges of modern life.

Although the cottage-garden style that has filtered down to us in the twenty-first century is something much softer and more carefree, the tradition of including vegetables, fruit and herbs mixed in amongst the flowers is still central to its spirit.

Original cottage gardens were never planned, and part of the secret of the good, modern cottage garden is that it should look as though it has grown up organically without any obvious design to it. It is the planting that creates the illusion of carefree abandon, not the layout.

Some key elements

Plan the garden around large borders, ideally flanking a path that you can wander down, with colour and scent accompanying you all the way. At its simplest, this can be a narrow path down the centre of the garden, with borders that take up all the space right to the edges – and that is how I had my own garden in London some 30 years ago.

Small town gardens are ideal for this very simple layout but it is essential not to complicate the design. Keep it simple – a path, either straight or curved (I have a rule that paths that run through borders can twist and bend, but paths that are primarily designed to take you from A to B, should always be straight), and as narrow as is practicable, and with the entire rest of the garden cultivated and planted. That path has to arrive somewhere – a seat is ideal, perhaps beneath a rustic bower smothered with deliciously fragrant roses or honeysuckle.

There should be a sense of the plants taking over the garden, spilling over every path, up every inch of wall or fence and twining into any open window. A word of warning though: this only works for more than a season if the gardener is ruthless and cuts and pulls with unbending rigour. Otherwise the thugs take over and all your more precious plants get swamped.

Mix it up

There is no need for separate beds for vegetables or herbs. Having large borders makes it much easier to mix small trees, shrubs, flowers, herbs, fruit and vegetables in the true cottage-garden style. By planting the garden as a happy jumble, you avoid the concentration of pests and diseases that monoculture encourages.

Sweet peas can climb supportive wigwams next door to deliciously edible climbing beans. An apple tree can provide beautiful blossom in spring, structure in summer and, of course, fruit in autumn. Roses and redcurrants can rub shoulders in the border as easily as rhubarb and rheum. I have edged cottage-garden borders with parsley and red lettuce as well as with carnations and primulas.

Herbs like lavender, rosemary, sage, dill and fennel are all useful kitchen herbs that slip easily in amongst quintessential cottage-garden plants like foxgloves, aquilegias, alchemilla, pinks, hollyhocks, lupins, delphiniums, phlox and roses. Mint, however, is always best grown in a container as it can too easily spread and take over a border.

Colour

Cottage gardens demand a distinct softness of tone. Pinks, lemon yellows, lavender, mauve, pale blues and white should dominate the palette. Many of the traditional cottage-garden plants like roses, pinks, sweet Williams, snapdragons, hollyhocks, delphiniums, lupins and phlox are all naturally within this range of colours and just by selecting them you set the palette for the garden.

Cottage-garden planting makes a soft jumble of textures and colours »

Pink is the key colour in soft, gentle planting schemes and there are more pink flowers than any other kind to select from. Some of my favourites, such as aquilegias, bleeding hearts, lupins, pink cranesbills like *Geranium endressii*, *G. riversleaianum* 'Russell Prichard' and *G.* x *oxonianum* 'Claridge Druce', and pink peonies and oriental poppies – are all archetypal cottage-garden plants.

Mix blue with pink and let the spectrum between them of mauves and lilacs have full rein, and you cannot help but capture the true cottage-garden spirit. Campanulas, knapweed, nepeta and *Anchusa* 'Loddon Royalist' are all good blue perennials. A good blue clematis like *Clematis* 'Perle d'Azure' can be allowed to scramble through a rose or other shrub and then be pruned back hard each spring. Delphiniums are a must, and the Elatum hybrids are perhaps easiest to grow.

If the site is well drained and sunny, then the bearded iris works as a true cottage-garden plant. And if you have heavy soil like I do, *Iris sibirica* will grow happily in a border.

Shrubs

Flowering shrubs are a key element in any cottage-garden border and lilac, philadelphus, potentilla, buddleia, lavender and clematis all mix well with a wide range of herbaceous and annual plants. If you have a shady area, hydrangeas will thrive. Clematis grow surprisingly well in shade. Although there should be a wide and eclectic mix of plants, cottage gardens are not the place for exotica like cannas, bamboos or bananas. The idea is to capture the spirit of the English countryside in full bloom – even if in practice that involves using plants from all over the world.

Perennials

Spring perennials are important because they perform at a time of year when there is not so much competition for space. So primroses, hellebores, pulmonarias, cranesbills, Solomon's seal, euphorbias and, especially, aquilegias, should be welcomed. In summer, peonies, delphiniums, lupins, lavatera and phlox are all perennials that we grow as much for the way that they make us and our gardens feel more tranquil and softly rural, as for the way that they look so pretty.

Summer herbaceous perennials like oriental poppies, phlox, campanulas, nepeta, delphiniums, wallflowers, peonies, alchemilla, asters, cardoons and helianthus look good in great drifts and clumps that can be cut back as they fade, when annuals or vegetables can be added to plug the gaps.

Climbers

Climbing the walls and through bushes should be honeysuckle and clematis, perhaps a rose or two and a wisteria. Choose varieties that are free-flowering, fragrant and fulsome, even if this means filling your garden with very common plants. The whole point of a cottage garden is to create sensual delight based upon utilitarian simplicity. It is not to show off rare or unusual plants.

Annuals and biennials

Annuals and biennials have an important part to play in any cottage garden and can be very easily and cheaply grown from seed. Snapdragons, sweet peas, sunflowers, lavatera, nigella, alyssum, cornflowers, larkspur and marigolds are all hardy annuals that can be simply sprinkled onto the soil in spring, direct where they are to flower, and allowed to weave amongst more permanent planting. They avoid all the expense of raising seedlings under cover.

Annuals and biennials have an important part to play in any cottage garden

Annual poppies, from magnificent opium poppies, yellow Welsh poppies and Shirley poppies, are superb and will pop up in future years having seeded themselves – often in unlikely places. But these random delights are in tune with all that is lovely about the cottage garden.

Half-hardy annuals like cosmos, tobacco plants and annual pinks must be raised with a little protection but a windowsill or small greenhouse is enough to grow hundreds of plants at any one time, and once the risk of frost is past, they can be planted out and will flower right until the first frosts of autumn.

Biennials are tough, quick but not flashy, and tend to seed themselves with abandon

Biennials are tough, quick but not flashy, and tend to seed themselves with abandon. Forget-me-nots, wallflowers, sweet Williams, Canterbury bells, foxgloves – both white and purple – honesty, Brompton stocks, pansies, and sweet rocket can all join the easy jumble of a cottage-garden border. You can either buy young plants in spring or autumn, or save money by sowing seed in spring and raising the plants to put into position in autumn ready for flowering next year.

Bulbs, corms and tubers

Bulbs such as snowdrops, crocuses, hyacinths, fritillaries, Solomon's seal, summer snowflakes, daffodils, tulips and alliums are essential, and later in the year, lilies (especially the Madonna lily), crocosmia, gladioli and dahlias are an important part of the planting balance.

Try and weave them through the borders, or use them in containers so they can be moved to where you most enjoy them, then move them to one side after they have done their bit.

Some of these, like tulips, dahlias and gladioli, can and will have garish, vibrant colours that seem at odds with the ethos of the cottage garden, but it is not an exercise in tightly controlled good taste. Bright colours are welcome as long as they act to set off the whole and do not unbalance it.

« Cow parsley froths in the Spring Garden in May

The cottage garden at a glance

1. **Softness** is the key to all cottage gardens. This is best achieved by generous drifts and billows of plants and using soft, pastel colours.
2. **Mix** in all and every kind of plant cheek by jowl. Not only shrubs, perennials and annuals mingle together, but also fruit, herbs and vegetables can grow side by side in the same border.
3. **Go** for maximum cultivated space. Surround your seating area with plants. If you have a lawn, make it small and enclosed with borders.
4. **Grow** as much from seed as possible. Annuals and biennials are an important contribution to the cottage-garden style.
5. **Topiary** is another traditional element. Yew is ideal but any evergreen plant can be clipped and shaped. Be playful and witty with it.
6. **Choose** your hard surfaces carefully. Brick paths – especially recycled bricks – always look right. If your ground drains well, grass paths are also ideal. Avoid hard-edged modern surfaces like concrete pavers.
7. **Make** a bower, pergola or covered seating area that supports climbing roses, honeysuckle or clematis to create a flowery, fragrant retreat.
8. **Avoid** using exotic plants that stand out as unusual or dramatic. This is not the time to recreate the jungle! Everything should create a harmonious blend evoking a glorious English countryside.

The Exotic Garden

Ever since exotic plants from all over the world began to be brought back to this country from the beginning of the seventeenth century, British gardeners have yearned to grow them at home. Now that many of us can jet off and visit tropical paradises for ourselves, that urge to create our own exotic garden at home is stronger than ever. And it can be done, even in the coldest, most northern gardens.

Any holiday-maker to the tropics will notice just how vigorous growth is and how fast compared to the northern hemisphere. It is that green vitality that you have to tap into to create a garden that feels truly exotic.

That tropical lushness is to do with the combination of the heat of the sun, the intensity of light and the availability of water. The first two of these factors are beyond any gardener's control but if you have reasonable rainfall or can collect rainwater so you can water your key plants if there is drought, then you have a much wider and lusher selection to play with. But enriching your soil will help more than anything else.

It is perfectly possible to create an exotic effect with extremely hardy plants and I do this in my own garden. I use the giant foliage of *Hosta* 'Snowden' and *H. sieboldiana*, the height of the giant Scotch thistle, *Onopordum acanthium*, that can reach 15ft in a few months, and cardoons. Both these last two have astonishingly vigorous growth in May and June, and beautiful glaucous foliage that contrasts really well with the rampant foliage of the golden hop, *Humulus lupulus* 'Aureus'.

Acanthus is one of those plants that provides an overdose of brilliant lush green but comes with a health warning, for once established, it is all but impossible to get rid of from a border. This is especially true of *Acanthus mollis*, which is semi-evergreen, surviving all but the sharpest of winters, whereas *A. spinosus* is decidedly herbaceous and completely disappears between November and April. Both have huge, dramatic spires of flowers that rise up from the great scalloped swell of their shiny leaves.

If you then use large containers to position dramatic flowering plants, you immediately scale up the exotic temperature. *Brugmansia* works superbly well in this way, as do cannas, phormiums and even the humble dahlia. Growing them in pots also means that you can ensure the right kind of soil and drainage, and makes it easier to protect tender plants in winter.

....

Ferns

Dry shade is seen as a major problem for gardeners. But many ferns love it and create a richly exotic corner lurking in the shadows. Given protection from wind, the male or Buckler fern will grow almost anywhere, sending up croziers 3ft tall that smell of freshly cut hay, while golden shield fern, *Dryopteris affinis*, is another superbly statuesque fern that will grow equally well in sun or shade. As with all drought-tolerant plants, water them well for their first year until established.

Blechnum chilense is a very robust evergreen fern with leathery, dark-green fronds. Like the shuttlecock fern, *Matteuccia struthiopteris*, which needs damp conditions, it will establish a short trunk, similar to a mini tree fern.

In milder areas the real tree fern, *Dicksonia antarctica*, instantly creates the right atmosphere and mood. It will need protecting in winter and the best way to do this is to fold the ferns over the top of the stem and wrap it in fleece. Tree ferns have their roots on the stem so they like humid air rather than moist soil. A spray with a hose every few days in a dry spell should suffice.

....

Palms

The Chusan palm, *Trachycarpus fortunei*, always adds a very un-British element to any garden and sets the tone for the planting around it with

Eucomis bicolor growing in a pot on The Mound »

real élan, although it is the hardiest of all palms and will grow in a wide range of gardens. Good drainage will always improve its health and planting it in a sheltered spot will protect it from the wind.

The dwarf fan palm, *Chamaerops humilis*, is also very hardy and will form a shrubby clump that creates a good understorey. Again, good drainage and a sunny, sheltered position will help a great deal.

Cordyline australis is not a palm but looks like one, and certainly casts an exotic shade in any coastal or urban garden where the winter temperatures do not fall below –5°C. It needs plenty of water in summer but should be kept dry in winter. In good weather it will flower freely.

Bananas

With its enormous and, in the case of *Ensete ventricosum* 'Maurelii', deep chocolate and plum-coloured leaves, no single plant is more exotically dramatic than the banana. They demand lots of water, the richest growing conditions that you can create, are not hardy, and need a sheltered spot if they are not to be ripped to shreds by winds – but for all that I consider them essential in any would-be exotic garden.

The hardiest is *Musa basjoo* but it needs a protective wigwam of fleece in cold areas or, like *Ensete*, should be lifted and brought indoors for protection before the first frosts. For containers, a small banana like *Musa lasiocarpa*, which only reaches about 4ft but has wonderful, thick, glaucous leaves and is even hardier than *M. basjoo*, is a good choice.

Cannas

Their combination of vivid, flamboyant flowers and enormous and striking foliage makes cannas among the most dramatic plants in any garden. I particularly like the mixture of dark or striped foliage with brilliant flowers such as *Canna* 'Wyoming', which has orange flowers, *C.* 'Black Knight', which has red flowers or *C.* 'Durban', which has

« *Ensete* banana underplanted with blood grass – *Imperata cylindrica* 'Rubra' chocolate leaves and orange flowers.

Even if you live in a very mild area, cannas still need lifting and cutting back by mid-November to give them a rest or else they will not flower the following year. Their roots are fleshy and store enough food to take the plant through its dormant winter season. In this country that can be quite a long time because they are not frost-hardy and it is best not to plant them out till the last possible risk of frost has passed.

I pack the cut-back plants in spent potting compost or leafmould (vermiculite or even wood chips would do) in a large pot in a cool but frost-free shed, to keep them protected and alive but dormant over winter. They should not be allowed to dry out, so water them every few weeks. I then bring them out of storage as soon as growth appears in spring and from mid-April, I gradually harden them off before their final planting out at the end of May.

Cannas like being moist so they should always be generously mulched after planting and watered thoroughly. Each individual flower only lasts a few days but more will be produced from the same flower spike until there are no more buds.

The tree dahlia, *Dahlia imperialis*, will create a huge plant, reaching 15ft or more in rich soil, but it only flowers in late summer after a really good baking. This hardly diminishes its value as it grows anew like a young tree every year and new plants can be taken very easily from cuttings in spring. It is tender so needs lifting and bringing under cover over winter or protecting with straw or fleece in mild areas.

Exotic climbers

The trumpet vine, *Campsis radicans*, with its deep, orange-red trumpet shaped flowers, is one of the most exotic-looking of all the climbers that will cope with a temperate climate. Passion flower, *Passiflora*, is very hardy yet has extraordinary flowers that produce distinct bright orange, egg-shaped fruits. *P. caerulea* is one of the hardiest but only *P. edulis* is really edible. *Solanum crispum* has dark purple flowers in summer from a growth that scrambles up support. *S. c.* 'Glasnevin' is particularly dark.

As long as it has neutral to alkaline soil, *Trachelospermum jasminoides* flowers profusely on a sunny wall, and exudes a delicious jasmine scent. I grow the annual cup-and-saucer vine, *Cobaea scandens*, in containers, sowing seed in April and planting out in early June to flower from late July through to autumn. Morning glory, *Ipomoea*, has the same regime, with *I. tricolor* 'Heavenly Blue' making scores of brilliant blue flowers. The really exotic *I. nil* 'Chocolate' has dappled, deep plum-coloured, otherworldly flowers.

Exotic gardening in dry conditions

Dramatic, dry-loving plants like echiums, yuccas, cardoons, stipas, sedums and melianthus can all cope with drier conditions.

These are plants that have evolved to cope with very low levels of rainfall, so hate sitting in wet conditions. This means that the drainage has to be very good. If your soil is at all moisture-retentive, then you will have to add plenty of gravel or horticultural grit – but not extra organic matter as this will provoke too much lush growth.

Agapanthus adds drama and can be grown in containers or in the ground as long as the roots are fairly constricted, otherwise the plant will put more energy into its foliage than its flowers. *Melianthus major*, the honey flower, is one of my own favourites. This is worth growing for its glaucous foliage but in a sunny, protected corner it will produce deep red flower heads. The Californian tree poppy, *Romneya coulteri*, will grow to over 6ft with silvery grey foliage and huge white flowers.

New Zealand flax, *Phormium tenax*, is hardy to about –5°C and makes a superb centrepiece for a container or border. Of the grasses, all members of the stipa family thrive in dry, well-drained conditions but the most flamboyant is *Stipa gigantea* with its 8ft-high oaten flower heads that glow in the evening sun.

The giant sea kale, *Crambe cordifolia*, is superb at the back of a border and *Verbascum olympicum* will reach 9ft in its second year. Echiums grow just as big, with towers of tiny blue flowers. There are over 30 species of aeonium and they look equally good in a container or the border. Such plants work well as a really exotic display in the driest conditions.

The exotic garden at a glance

1. **Prepare** the soil well before planting. Get rid of any compaction by digging and adding as much organic material as you can get hold of – and then top this up every year with at least 2–3in of good organic mulch. Nothing else will help preserve the vibrant lushness that you are striving for.

2. **Create** shelter from prevailing winds. Plants with large leaves can be terribly damaged by wind, both structurally and in terms of growing stress, so good fences, hedges and walls are essential to create wind barriers and microclimates.

3. **Put** in an irrigation system or good rainwater storage. To achieve the lushness that a really exotic garden needs (save in dry conditions), there must be a steady supply of moisture. Generous mulching will help, but consider a drip-feed irrigation system both as a very efficient way of using water and to keep plants irrigated when you are not there.

4. **Buy** key dramatic plants and work round them. Spend your budget on fewer but bigger plants to create the right scale and effect, then infill around them. A few really stunning plants will always work better in this style of gardening than a mass of smaller ones.

5. **Do** not overlook hardy 'ordinary' border plants. A plant does not have to be tender, rare, difficult to grow or expensive to look truly exotic. Onopordums, cardoons, giant hostas and shuttlecock ferns used creatively can hold their own with plants from anywhere in the world.

6. **You** can create an exotic effect in a very dry garden but choose your plants appropriately and go for a consistent look.

7. **Be** prepared to store plants in a frost-free place over winter and have adequate winter protection for plants that are too big to be moved.

8. **Accept** that this style of garden is only at its best for half the year.

9. **Do** not be tentative – it is all or nothing.

A Modern Urban Garden

Gardening is by and large a conservative art, taking comfort from the past. But you can create a stylish modern garden that demands very little maintenance and yet is ideal for relaxing and entertaining in.

There are two ways of keeping maintenance to a minimum. The first is to use a lot of hard landscaping, which is relatively expensive to set up but once established needs very little upkeep. The second is to use plants that only need pruning or attending to once or twice a year, such as tightly clipped box or yew.

The modern garden is essentially hard-edged and free from whimsy. So use either regular stone with sharp cut edges or man-made slabs, pavers or setts of some sort. Symmetry, balance and order suit this style very well. The lines should remain clean and uncluttered, and this dictates the style of planting. The heart of this kind of garden is the sitting and eating area – the whole garden should lead to or revolve around this. It is a place to relax in rather than to spend a busy gardening weekend.

Plants

'Architectural' is the expression given to those plants that shape or frame a setting, and is the kind of planting that set-dresses an otherwise rather hard backdrop. There is a wide range of plants that will do this, from huge bananas to yuccas, agapanthus, tree ferns and cacti. The essential point is that they stand alone rather than being used as a component in the assembled harmony of a border.

In general, evergreen plants look constantly good throughout the year and can include flowering shrubs such as camellias, lavender, rosemary, myrtle, mahonia, ceanothus, escallonia, garrya, *Magnolia grandiflora*, griselinia and *Choisya ternata*. All these can be clipped or trained.

Plants that can be shaped into hedges and topiary, or can be used as cloud pruning, include yew, box, holly, *Ilex crenata*, privet and Portuguese laurel. These are ideal for a thoroughly modern and yet low-maintenance garden because one annual clip is all that they need to look trim the year round.

Bamboos work very well in the modern low-maintenance garden and as long as they do not dry out, need little attention. *Phyllostachys nigra* is the modernists' bamboo of choice and is set off well by pools or tanks of black water (see below) to match its black stems.

The modern garden is free from whimsy. The lines should remain clean and uncluttered, and this dictates the style of planting

For colour and drama, bulbs grown in pots work well. They can be moved into position when in flower and then set to one side as they die down and they will, in the main, dutifully reappear the following year.

Water

In a modern setting, very formal water features, with little or even no planting, can look both starkly chic or, if used with a pump, bring movement and the play of light that adds real interest to what might otherwise be rather an austere setting.

A very shallow formal pond, lined in black and edged with stone, will reflect light beautifully. I have seen a pond like this, edged on three sides with high, painted walls so that the reflections are constantly playing, and it was fascinating. Add water falling into the pool and exiting it so that you have the sound of water meeting water, and you have real vivacity.

Corten steel tanks that quickly rust make stylish water features and can be made to any size. Rushes, such as the delicate flowering rush *Butomus umbellatus*, have an architectural quality and irises, such as

Iris ensata, I. versicolor, I. laevigata and *I. pseudacorus*, all look superb rising simply from still water. These can all be planted in baskets and submerged onto the bottom of the pond.

Even a small rill can be enough to transform a garden. A rill is a very narrow strip of water, edged in stone or steel that runs along a path, so that you walk either side of it or across it. Again, it is almost maintenance-free once set up.

Wildlife Gardening

The best thing that you can do to encourage wildlife into your garden is to stop gardening. Let the lawn become a tussocky meadow and the borders strangle with weeds. Let brambles romp and nettles flourish. Hedges should go uncut and should fight it out with elder, self-sown ash and birch. If it looks like an abandoned railway siding, then the job is well done.

An immaculate garden is a hostile place to most wildlife. Beautifully weeded borders, with every fallen leaf and twig gathered and disposed of, hedges kept constantly crisp and grass mown to within a fraction of its life may make a certain sort of gardener glow with pride but will provide little comfort for most of our birds, mammals and insects.

If you want the natural world to share your garden, some compromises must be made. The goal is to learn to live together and accommodate one another without sacrificing colour, productivity or design.

But anyone, wherever they live, can have a garden that is both beautiful and rich with a varied mix of wildlife. And there is a growing need for this because, as agricultural land becomes, increasingly, a species-poor monoculture, most gardens are more wildlife-friendly than the average field.

It is astonishing how much birdlife will be added to a small garden simply by planting some deciduous hedging and a selection of deciduous and evergreen shrubs. If you have room for a small tree or two, then so much the better. Most gardens are, by default, rich hunting grounds for a huge range of creatures.

But the gardener must try not to be blindly selective about what constitutes acceptable 'wildlife'. Slugs, moles, rabbits, urban foxes and mosquitoes are all wildlife, too. Many creatures that seem harmful to your immediate garden might be an integral part of the food chain, enabling the more obviously beautiful birds or mammals to exist.

Although there are occasions when the caterpillars munching through your brassicas or the slug that has devastated your hostas might simply be classed as the enemy, in almost all circumstances they are part of a much bigger, much richer picture than your isolated garden problems.

Learn to see the garden as a holistic entity of which you, just like every other living creature, are just one small component. So start by not using pesticides, herbicides or fungicides. Chemicals are not selective. Good examples are the insecticides that kill aphids – they will also damage pollinators. Do not use a sledgehammer to crack a nut.

Respect, care and a delight in the incredible richness of nature is the key to a healthy and fascinating garden. Each predator must have enough to feed on to maintain its controlling presence. So you need some aphids if you are to have ladybirds or lacewings, and you need some slugs if hedgehogs, beetles and toads are to remain to eat them. It is an entirely self-regulating system and it works fine.

It is astonishing how much birdlife will be added to a small garden simply by planting some hedging and a selection of shrubs

Having stopped blasting your plants with chemicals, there are a few simple but very effective measures you can take. The first thing I would recommend is to allow an area of grass to grow long. Have at least a patch that you cut just twice a year, in July and October. Apart from anything else, this will encourage wild flowers (even if they are only daisies, dandelions and buttercups), which will increase insect diversity. Diversity is more important than the actual number of any one species. A healthy garden has as wide a range of insects, birds and mammals as possible, rather than trophy-hunting the rarity of one or two specimens.

A mixed hedge of native species with hazel, dogwood, hawthorn, blackthorn and guelder rose provides nesting cover for birds and insects and also produces nectar from its flowers. I suggest planting plenty of groundcover beneath as it is particularly good for small mammals and invertebrates. Lamium, geranium, vinca and ivy all combine to make a dense and protective layer.

Best flowers for bees and pollinators: Agastache, alliums, asters, campanulas, cornflower, cosmos, evening primrose, geum, hardy geraniums, hollyhock, mallow, scabious, wild clary

Best shrubs for bees and pollinators: Buddleia, ceanothus, cotoneaster, lilac, mahonia, shrub roses

Best trees for bees and pollinators: All fruit trees, blackthorn, chestnut, hawthorn, hazel, ornamental cherry

Top 10 nectar plants for butterflies: *Aster* x *frickartii*, aubretia, *Buddleia davidii*, 'Oregon Thornless' blackberry (this is, as the name suggests, less prickly than the wild form), field scabious, French marigold, lavender, marjoram, red valerian, *Sedum spectabile*

Wildlife pond

A pond, designed to look as natural as possible, will instantly attract every kind of wildlife into your garden, including frogs, newts, insects, birds, bats and mammals. All of these will actively contribute to the environmental health of your plants as well as providing you with another tier of interest and pleasure.

Do not worry about 'stocking' the pond in any way – just create the right environment and animals will come. The planting that best suits this kind of naturalistic water feature is also one of the most beautiful and charming of any kind of gardening.

Making a pond is easy – you dig a hole, line it with some kind of water-retentive material, then fill it with water. That is it. Finessing it involves hiding the liner with stones and planting, and incorporating

Removing dead vegetation from the pond »

shelves for varying depths of water for different types of plants as well as for creating different aquatic habitats.

One of the distinctive features of a dedicated wildlife pond is its beach. If you incorporate an area of very gently sloping bank, then you provide both an easy entry and a vital exit for almost any creature, from a water boatman to a thirsty hedgehog. You can easily do this by grading the soil under the liner and using stones, cobbles and finally washed grit to make a very shallow area that arrives at larger stones half-submerged in the water. The beach area should be left free of plants but can take up as little as a fifth of the circumference of the pond itself.

A pond, designed to look as natural as possible, will instantly attract every kind of wildlife into your garden, including frogs, newts, insects, birds, bats and mammals

An old log might not be your idea of aquatic beauty, but to encourage wildlife, it is a good idea to add one to your pond. Just let it float and very slowly decompose in the water. Beetles love it and frogs will perch on it to bask in the sun.

An area of long grass and nettles around the perimeter of the pond provides good cover as well as being caterpillar fodder for a range of butterflies such as red admirals, tortoiseshells, peacocks and commas.

Marginal planting, both in and outside the pond, serves as ideal cover for a range of animals. In fact, cover of all kinds is good even if it looks 'messy' to the fastidious horticultural eye, so don't worry about algae, duckweed or keeping your pond clean and clear. Even a stagnant puddle is a rich resource for wildlife and is far better than no water at all. Apart from anything else, water tends to self-regulate and respond to weather and the seasons without any human help.

Making a pond

Choose a site that gets direct sunlight for at least half the day.

A round pond or one with flowing curves is likely to look more natural than a square or rectangular one. Allow plenty of room around the pond for planting.

Mark out the outline of the pond using string and canes or a hosepipe. Allow for marginal plants by including shallow shelves around the perimeter. Remember to make a section of the circumference extremely shallow to form a beach.

Aquatic plants such as water lilies need deeper water, so aim to include a section that is at least 3ft deep. Even a small hole takes quite a few barrowloads of soil to excavate, so plan what you will do with the waste soil – ideally incorporate it into the garden.

Check that the edges are all level. Use wooden pegs and a spirit level and be exact because the water will instantly expose any inaccuracy. If the site is sloping, then you will have to build up one side. Avoid steep slopes falling down into or away from the edge of the pond.

When you are satisfied with the shape and size of the pond, remove any stones or roots, and firm and smooth the soil. If you are using a rigid liner this can then be fitted into the hole and the soil backfilled around the edges. If you are using a flexible liner, first line the surface of the soil with geotextile underlay, carpeting underfelt or an inch of sand. Do not stint on this because whatever you use, the purpose is the same: to protect the lining from being punctured.

Calculate the size of liner you need by measuring the longest distances along the length and breadth of the pond, then add twice the maximum depth to both measurements. So a pond 10ft x 6ft at its widest points and 3ft at its deepest will need a liner at least 16ft x 12ft.

Stretch the liner gently over the pool area and let it ease itself into all the contours, gathering it into folds to avoid creases. Do not start to add water until you are happy that the liner has as few wrinkles as possible. Leave plenty of excess liner, particularly under the beach area and hold the excess liner securely down with bricks or stones. Fill with water, pulling any creases free. Although the water will stretch the liner as it fills, ensuring a tight fit, it will also hold any creases in place.

When the pond is completely full, leave it for 24 hours to ensure it is watertight, then trim the liner, leaving at least a foot to spare all the way round. Finally, add stones, soil and plants to hide the liner and create a natural-looking pond.

Planting a pond

A wildlife pond does not need any particular planting as long as there is plenty of cover both around and in the pond.

Hostas, ligularias, cornus, *Gunnera manicata*, rheums, rodgersias, astilbes and irises will all thrive around the margins of the pond and in boggy areas. Purple loosestrife will grow anywhere it can get its feet into water, as will the lovely bright yellow marsh marigold. Plant as naturally as possible and do not be too tidy. A tangle of growth at the water's edge will provide perfect cover.

Some of our native wildflowers thrive best in very wet conditions away from competition with grass. These include marsh marigold, meadow buttercup, yellow loosestrife, comfrey, cuckoo flower, flag iris and greater bird's foot trefoil.

For a wildlife pond, do not add fish as they eat tadpoles. And if you use a pump, it should be very small and disturb the water as little as possible because frogs only lay their eggs in still, shallow water.

Grass and wildflower meadows

A wildflower meadow can look as beautiful as any herbaceous border, but the flowers in it make surprisingly little difference to the quality of wildlife. It is long grass that is the key to a healthy and varied insect population. Even one square yard will make a big difference.

But if you want to go the whole hog, just mow a narrow path down the centre of your lawn and leave the rest to become a glorious wildflower meadow, with plants such as cowslips, kidney vetch, lady's bedstraw, ox-eye daisy, field scabious, knapweed and meadow cranesbill

« The pond is surrounded by lush cover that is ideal for wildlife

91

growing in amongst the grass.

Rather than a true wildflower meadow – which can be tricky to sustain as it requires very low soil fertility – it is easier to plant spring-flowering bulbs into the grass. This means that a range of bulbs can be seen before the grass begins to grow. Snowdrops, crocuses, daffodils and species tulips all naturalise well in grass. If the ground is moist, snakeshead fritillaries and camassias look superb. Since the flowers die back by mid-spring, the grass will start to grow long and hide the untidiness of the bulbs as they die. The fresh new grass itself can look wonderful at this stage in the year.

Then, some time in July or August – but never before midsummer – the grass can be cut. It is important to rake it up and take it to the compost heap, as any cut grass left on the ground will only feed the grass at the expense of the flowers. If your compost bin is too small for the grass cuttings, just make a heap in a corner somewhere and let it quietly compost down – becoming another haven for insect life as it does so.

You can then mow the grass regularly just like a normal lawn, as long as you collect the grass when you do so or let it grow long again before giving it a second cut and rake any time before Christmas. Either way, the grass should go into winter as short as possible. This routine will maximise the chance for wild flowers to thrive in amongst the grass, adding to what will be, in my opinion, as beautiful as any neatly mown lawn – and much more environmentally friendly.

Birds

The song of a blackbird or thrush is as beautiful as the most perfect rose and, I think, an essential component of any good garden. But to get thrushes and blackbirds to visit, you must have food for them in the shape of worms – for which you need healthy, organically rich soil – as well as invertebrates and insects of all kinds.

And to encourage birds, in addition to having a wide selection of flowers, long grass and water, you need trees. These not only provide cover and nesting sites but are also a potential environment for a wide range of wildlife. But you must choose wisely. The London plane, for example, apparently only supports one British insect species, whereas the pedunculate oak (*Quercus robur*) supports 284. I know that some people are hesitant to plant an oak tree in their garden because they think that it is too 'slow' or that it will not truly become an oak in their lifetime. This is a big mistake. It is lovely from the first and gives enormous pleasure as it grows – as well as encouraging wildlife.

Watching birds is one of the great pleasures of the winter garden. Put out food for them, preferably out of reach of cats, and with some of it protected by a mesh with small enough holes to keep out pigeons, starlings and predators such as sparrow hawks, but with big enough holes for tits, finches and other small song birds to feed in safety.

Irregular feeding can do more harm than good so it is important that once you start to put food out – sunflower seeds, grubs, breadcrumbs and any fat make the best all-round mix – you continue to do so until well into spring as they can waste a lot of energy flying to your bird table unless that energy can be replaced when they arrive.

Nestboxes also encourage birds into the garden. Tits need a box with a round hole placed about 9ft above ground in a sheltered spot, whereas robins like a more open box in a very tucked-away spot such as behind a climber or at the back of a shed.

Insects

Insects are less conspicuous and less glamorous than songbirds, dragonflies or hedgehogs but are the foundation from which a healthy wildlife garden is built. The American word 'bugs' contributes to a profound misunderstanding of the importance of insects as part of the chain of life. The more varied a garden's insect population, the healthier it will be. Without a healthy insect population, the whole food chain of birds, mammals and flowers starts to fall apart. Not only do we want more insects – we need them.

Bees

It has been estimated that 80 per cent of the western diet is dependent upon pollination by bees, so without bees, the human race would rapidly starve and probably become extinct. Their steady decline is therefore a cause for real alarm.

The cause of this decline seems to be a combination of things. The varroa mite has become a major pest, attacking bees at every stage of their life cycle. It sucks the blood of adults and weakens them, making them more susceptible to viral infections. Add to that increasing evidence that agricultural pesticides are harming bees, and you have a potentially disastrous situation.

But gardens are a rich source of food for bees and with a little care, they can be made more rich without any trouble or loss of pleasure to the gardener. We can actively – and, importantly, should – nurture and conserve the British bee population.

You can select plants that not only look terrific but are also particularly attractive to bees. Recent research has concluded that it does not matter where a plant comes from in order to be suitable for bees, so there is no need to focus solely on native species, but how accessible its nectar is does make a big difference.

Thus any plant that is open and simple, such as members of the daisy family, or any that are set on a 'bobble', such as scabious and members of the thistle family, are always going to be ideal. Bumblebees have longer tongues so are better adapted for plants that are more funnel-shaped, such as foxgloves.

Bees also love fruit trees – in fact they love any flowering trees – and they go, too, for all legumes, such as peas, beans, clover and sweet peas. Add to those, dandelions, blackberries, asters, ivy and willow.

Remember that bees need pollen and the smaller flowers of unhybridised species are likely to be a much richer source of this than huge show blooms on plants that are the result of elaborate breeding.

Honeybees need pollen as close to their hive as possible but they do not need variety. So sequential monoculture, such as fruit blossom in spring followed by a field of rape or heather on a mountainside, suits them perfectly.

For the gardener, this means making sure that you plant in some quantity so the bees have plenty of what they like in a seamless succession for as much of the flowering year as possible. Planting in blocks and drifts rather than dotting odd bits and pieces around the garden is what works.

Bumblebees are more inclined to graze and will happily go from plant to plant, nibbling a little here and sipping a bit there, with less of the furious business of honeybees. They will happily work their way round your garden without the same need for plant volume and succession.

Wildlife gardening at a glance

1. **Avoid** tidiness: leave leaves, patches of weeds, overgrown shrubs and climbers, and dead stems on plants. All this provides essential cover and shelter for insects, birds and small mammals like bats. Create winter cover for larger mammals like hedgehogs by gathering bundles of sticks and leaving in a pile against a fence or shed.
2. **You** must include water in the garden, even if it is only a birdbath. A small pond with plenty of marginal planting and a shallow approach in one section to enable creatures to crawl in and out is ideal.
3. **Cultivate** your weeds where they do not conflict with decorative plants. Many weeds are important food plants, for example, nettles are vital to butterflies such as red admirals, small tortoiseshells and peacocks, whose caterpillars feed on them.
4. **Long** grass is essential. Leave a patch of lawn unmown until at least midsummer. Cut and rake it to encourage wildflowers. Underplant with bulbs like crocus for a brilliant spring display that will also provide pollen for early insects.
5. **Monoculture** is not good for wildlife even though it may create a dramatic display for the human eye. Grow a wide range of flowers with open, accessible shapes and as long a flowering season as possible to provide a good supply of pollen and nectar for insects.

6. **Avoid** all pesticides, insecticides, herbicides and fungicides. Using them to kill specific pests is like using a shotgun to kill a fly and will not only destroy many beneficial organisms, but will also set up a chain reaction of plagues of problems. Strive to help create a balanced environment that is self-regulating.

7. **Only** cut your hedges out of the nesting season – between October and December is ideal for deciduous hedges. Those that must be cut twice should be cut as lightly as possible for their second trim.

8. **A** selection of umbellifers such as angelica, fennel, chervil and dill, all of which are rich in nectar, is particularly attractive to hoverflies and lacewings, whose larvae in turn eat aphids.

9. **Not** only does compost recycle all your waste material from house and garden and enrich your soil, but it also enhances the bacterial and fungal life in your garden, and this is the base upon which all other, much more visible, forms of wildlife will build.

Children

Create an area in the garden dedicated to the children that is safe and always theirs, and do not shunt it to the far end of the garden – small children always want to be near the house.

A play area does not have to sit like an ungainly intruder in the garden. It can be horticulturally inspired. Paddling pools can be ponds and sand pits beaches. Overgrown shrubs can be dens or dens can be constructed from living plant material like willow.

Make a treehouse, shed or building of some kind that is exclusively for children. Buying a ready-made one is good but making it yourself, however badly, is much more fun and the children will treasure it more.

Never try and make children into gardeners – that will happen in its own good time – but do encourage them to love the garden

A lawn is essential but forget the perfect sward. It must be tough enough to take lots of wear and tear. This means using ryegrass and putting time and effort into ensuring good drainage to minimise compaction.

Grow as many fruits and vegetables as possible. Make harvesting a treat for the children and try and eat something from the garden as often as you can.

Never try and make children into gardeners – that will happen in its own good time. But try very hard to make them love your shared family garden because that is the fount of all good gardening.

And remember, plants can be replaced. Childhood only happens once and must be nurtured as the most precious part of any garden.

Containers

Pots add drama, a sense of staging, variety and an architectural structure that works with any kind of planting, from a sprinkle of annual daisies to large trees. Every garden of every size and shape, and in any situation or location, is improved by having plenty of plants growing in pots.

They can be positioned exactly where a plant most thrives and then moved according to the season or simply your whim. And pots give you an invaluable element of control over growing conditions such as soil type. So for example, in my neutral to alkaline soil, I can grow rhododendrons and camellias in pots in an ericaceous potting mix.

Big pots can become mini-borders or flower arrangements in their own right, combining shrubs, perennials, annuals and bulbs that grow and develop, and provide fresh interest for up to half the year.

Pots can also enable you to muster a seasonal display that can look terrific for a short while and then, when the pots have finished flowering, can be moved out of the limelight, where they can scruffily die back into exhausted dormancy while another set of plants in pots takes their place.

And if you have a balcony, flat roof or even windowsill, then not only is there an opportunity for growing in containers, but the containers become your garden and can give just as much pleasure as any border.

As long as the container has some drainage and an opening at the widest part of the vessel, then absolutely anything that will hold soil and take regular watering can be pressed into service. Barrels have long been cut in half and used for larger displays. Metal pots can be sleek and chic but they can come in the form of recycled buckets and bathtubs. Stone sinks and troughs are shallow but attractive and are

We use the table outside the potting shed to create
a vibrant seasonal display of massed pots »

98

especially good for alpines that have shallow roots. I have seen old tea chests, washing-up bowls, drainage pipes, chimneys, dustbins, old baskets, saucepans, cooking-oil containers, a redundant pair of boots and an upturned hat all successfully used for growing a wide range of plants from tulips to turnips, with all, in their own way, looking good.

Potting-compost mixes

My very intensive jewel-coloured planting needs plenty of goodness so I make up a potting mixture designed to nourish it right through the summer. This consists of equal measures of bought-in peat-free potting compost, sieved leafmould, sieved garden compost and horticultural grit to ensure drainage. I mix it all up in a wheelbarrow and over the years I have found that big, hungry plants thrive on it. However, a good peat-free potting compost will work fine as long as you supplement it with a weekly liquid feed (see below).

But herbs or Mediterranean plants like lavender, santolina, cistus and pelargoniums need a much weaker mixture with very fast drainage to thrive. I would mix a peat-free (and it is essential that you do not use a peat-based compost for these plants as they need alkalinity), bark- or coir-based compost with up to its own volume again in horticultural grit. This will make it very free-draining and will reduce the nutrients – which are exactly the conditions that these plants love. They will still need watering at least weekly, and a fortnightly feed would do no harm.

Fresh compost must be used for every sowing or planting, and any crops that will be growing for more than a couple of months will need feeding.

When a plant needs a bigger pot, try and go up just one size so that there is no more than 2in of soil between the edge of the rootball and the inside of the new container. This will avoid the excess potting compost acting as a sump for water.

When using a liquid feed, resist any temptation to make the mixture richer. Plants can only absorb so much feed at a time and it should be used as a top up rather than to induce a spurt of growth, which will only result in weak shoots that will attract aphids and fungal problems. Strong, steady growth is the ideal.

Drainage

All containers need drainage holes. Many plastic pots and window boxes are sold without any drainage holes in them, so these must be drilled out, in the base. Make sure the holes are at least half an inch wide and err on the side of too many rather than too few. There is some debate about the need for crocks (a layer of broken pieces of pot, pebbles or even polystyrene chips) but I always use them if only to stop the compost falling through drainage holes – which on some larger terracotta pots can be quite big.

If you have your pots on a roof or balcony, they will have to be stood on a tray of sorts, to collect the drips, but make sure that the pot itself is not standing in the water as this will negate the effects of the drainage. Raise it up on feet of some kind. Another way round this is to drill drainage holes an inch or so up from the base of the pot and then make sure that the pot is filled with crocks to above the holes so that the water never rises above that level.

Watering

Watering too much is a bigger problem than watering too little. Poor drainage, followed by erratic watering, are the biggest causes of poor growth. As a rule, a good soak once a week is enough for most plants, save in very warm weather.

It is far better to water very thoroughly once a week than to give a shower every day. In fact, daily, light watering can reduce water uptake, especially in hot weather, because the water does not penetrate deeply into the soil, which encourages the roots to grow to the surface, where they dry out much more rapidly than roots that have to delve deep for their moisture.

A plant in a pot will need more water than its garden-planted counterpart and a large, fast-growing one much more. I water our pots until the water going in at the top seems to be coming out equally fast at the bottom. If this happens too quickly, it means that either the drainage is too free or, more probably, that the plant is potbound and dried up, and there is not enough soil in the container to absorb any water. In this case, submerge the pot in a bucket of water until the bubbles stop rising. This may take a good half hour if the soil is very dry. Then repot the plant in something bigger so there is soil for the roots to grow into.

Irrigation systems are expensive and can be fiddly to set up but they save time and are essential if you are away much. They have individual lines going into each container from a ring hose, and drip water slowly onto the soil directly around the roots of each plant. This ensures that there is minimal evaporation, no splashing and no water damage to flowers, fruit or leaves, and much less water is used than in overhead watering.

Never fill a pot to the brim with compost or mulch, otherwise water just splashes off it, especially when it is dry. Leave a good inch for water to make a puddle before soaking in.

Container trouble

Plants grown in containers can seem especially attractive to pests and vulnerable to disease. This is almost entirely due to the almost unavoidable fact that anything grown in a container is likely to be more stressed than the same plant grown in the soil. It will have access to less water and nutrients, or be overwatered and overfed, and is often more exposed to cold, wind and excess sun, especially on a roof. Hostas are an excellent example. I grow lots of hostas in my borders and have hardly any slug damage at all. But I have a single pot planted with *Hosta undulata* var. *albomarginata* that is always ravaged by the end of summer – even though exactly the same variety grows untouched a yard away. So either choose plants that will thrive in any given position, or place the container where your chosen plants will be happiest.

Overfeeding will encourage soft, lush growth that is a magnet for sap-sucking insects like aphids as well as slugs and snails. The idea is to grow healthy plants, which does not mean that they are extra-large or floriferous but that they are resilient and well adapted to whatever position they are in.

Vine weevils are often introduced into gardens via plants bought in containers at garden centres. It is worth lifting any plant from its pot before buying, and checking the roots to make sure that no vine weevils are there.

Containers for shade

Even the deepest shade can hold a container planted with ferns and ivy, and look mysterious and dramatic. However most shady spots have some sunlight so what you plant will depend upon the time of day when the containers are shadiest.

Even the deepest shade can hold a container planted with ferns and ivy, and look mysterious and dramatic

Morning shade is a protective shroud for plants such as camellias that are easily damaged by bright sunlight on frozen petals, causing the petals to thaw too fast and burst their cells. Shade in midday stops pale colours burning out and all but the most heat-loving plants will prefer shelter from the noon sun.

Evening shade is good for white flowers that attract moths rather than butterflies to pollinate them and are likely to smell exceptionally strong and fragrant.

A container planted with a woodland plant mix of *Alchemilla mollis*, *Euphorbia amygdaloides* var. *robbiae* and heuchera, along with the trailing strands of *Vinca minor* will be perfectly happy as long as it gets a few hours of sun a day and does not dry out too much.

Acanthus mollis and *A. spinosus* look superb in a large pot – we have two spectacular examples growing out of an old galvanised bathtub, even though it is placed in deep shade. Both seem to thrive in it

although perhaps *A. spinosus* is a better choice, if very dry.

Ferns are a useful and beautiful solution to dry shade and look handsome in pots. *Dryopteris filix-mas* will grow seemingly untroubled by lack of moisture or light. Soft shield fern is also particularly drought-resistant and most of the adiantum and polypodium ferns will do fine, too. The potting compost soil should ideally be split half and half with leafmould (not compost) to reduce fertility and although drought-tolerant, these ferns will need watering weekly.

Maximum use from big pots

I have four large pots in the centre of our Jewel Garden that I always plant in autumn with tulips for a brilliant April display. I plant wallflowers over the top of them so the bulbs push up through the wallflower growth, and the result is a fiery display that lasts into mid-May. Then these are removed, the wallflowers composted and the tulips lined out in a corner of the garden to die back and be replanted for cut flowers next year. (I recommend buying fresh tulip bulbs each year for containers to produce the best flowering display.) Then I replant the pots for an arrangement that will last through to November. This means having a strong central plant that will give structure, a mid-layer to provide bulk and an understorey that can spill and twine as well as flower continuously.

Pots offer a superb chance to try things out, make combinations and create dramatic effects – for a season at a time. This obviously applies to hanging baskets, window boxes and tubs, just as it does to any large container that looks best with more than one plant.

Design tips

The key to using containers as part of a larger garden – as opposed to on a roof or balcony, where they are the garden – is to keep them in

« Big pots like these in the Jewel Garden demand dramatic planting that can be renewed at least once in the growing season

context with everything around them. It is a mistake to think of a pot as a wholly independent flower arrangement. It needs to work with its surroundings – including the colours and textures of the building – just as much as any shrubs or herbaceous plants in a border.

But containers do not have to be instead of or separate from a border. A good-sized pot set in a border, perhaps raised on a plinth of some kind, adds variety and texture as well as enabling you to use plants that are perhaps not suited to your soil as part of the overall border planting scheme.

Just because a container is big, it does not mean that it looks good if you pack it with lots of plants. Like a good flower arrangement, the secret is to have a relatively limited choice of plants that harmonise in colour, shape and growing habit.

A large container is also the best way to focus the eye where you want it to go, either at the end of a vista – a pair of pots flanking a path, entrance or focal point create a real sense of expectation – or as any kind of a diversion that perhaps surprises and detains you. The smaller your garden, the more effective this is.

Larger containers such as tubs are ideal for growing climbers, shrubs or even small trees. I have grown climbing roses, clematis, hawthorns, Portuguese laurel and acers in pots that have flourished for years, as well as citrus, bay and large rosemary bushes.

A few really large pots make a space look bigger whereas lots of small ones can seem cluttered

Large pots are also ideal for annual climbers such as sweet peas, the cup-and-saucer vine, black-eyed Susan and morning glory, using a temporary wigwam of canes to support the growth. But it is important to replace the compost at the end of the growing season as the plants will have used up every available scrap of nutrients.

A few really large pots make a space look bigger whereas lots of small ones can seem cluttered, though a cluster of smaller pots that are changed and replanted seasonally focussed around a more permanently positioned large one always looks good, and the repetition of the same plant individually planted in a row of small pots – I use snowdrops, primroses, crocus, lavender and pelargoniums in this way – looks really terrific.

Container growing at a glance

1. **Group** containers together for massed appeal either in a bunch or symmetrically flanking a path or lining a wall. Small pots repeated can make a big impression.
2. **Large** pots are focal points that draw the eye. Use them dramatically as a theatrical performance.
3. **Change** the planting with the seasons. A good pot is expensive and should earn its keep for as long as possible. Have at least two different plant combinations a year.
4. **Never** reuse old potting compost as all the goodness in it will be used up.
5. **Do** not overwater and always ensure good drainage. A heavy soak once a week is better than a daily sprinkle.
6. **Pots** exposed to the wind will dry out much more quickly than those with some shelter. Hanging baskets are particularly vulnerable as are window boxes and roof gardens. Grouping pots together will provide a lot of protection and slow evaporation.
7. **Do** not overfeed. A dilute feed high in potash will help develop strong roots and flowers. Avoid feeds high in nitrogen as they only encourage lush growth that attracts pests and disease.

Climbers

One of the ways of making the most of available garden space is by using the third dimension and going up as much as possible. A garden with lots of height is always much more interesting – and environmentally rich – than one spread out flat like a carpet.

In the medium term, this means planting small trees, using tripods and frames for climbers, and choosing flowering plants – even very ordinary ones such as delphiniums, hollyhocks, verbascums and sunflowers – for their ability to grow fast and tall.

Most houses have at least one wall that can be planted against and most gardens have a wall or fence around the outside. These are all ideal for training climbers against. You can also easily erect fences and walls within the garden – however small it might be – that immediately provide two more vertical planes to grow plants against. In fact, many small gardens have more vertical growing space than horizontal.

It is a truth that plants will grow almost anywhere but if you want to make the best of the resources you have, then you must choose those plants that will thrive rather than merely survive where you plant them. The smaller the space available, the more it is worth taking trouble with your choice. Where you have room for six plants of a theme or colour, it hardly matters if one fails. Where space only permits one specimen and that goes pear-shaped, then it blows the whole garden apart.

Working with the compass points

It is vital to know the compass points in relation to your garden – and especially so for climbers. A south-facing wall will be on the north side of the house or garden. It gets the full effect of the sun from

Clematis 'Etoile Violette' in full glory in the Jewel Garden »

mid-morning until early evening, which is 9am till 3pm in winter and 10am till about 7pm in summer. The cold winds, from north and east, will not touch it. It is sunny, hot and dry. The base of any wall, even after quite heavy rain, is a dry place. Brick or stone suck up moisture from the ground as well as deflecting a lot of rain. So any plant against a south wall needs extra irrigation and mulching.

Many slightly tender plants will thrive – wisteria, jasmine, some roses, most fruit, ceanothus, eccremocarpus, stephanotis and trachelospermum. But most clematis (with the exception of the very early-flowering *Clematis balearica* and the evergreen *C. armandii*) as well as honeysuckles and some roses will find it too hot and dry.

A north-facing wall will be in shade for most of the time and certainly during the central part of the day. But this is not in itself a problem although the range of plants that enjoy growing in shade is limited. They all tend to have white or very pale flowers for the obvious reason that this makes them more visible for would-be pollinators.

Clematis 'Moonlight' fades to practically tissue colour in full sun, whereas it retains a strong white glow in shade. I have a *C. montana* that is perfectly happy on its north wall and the flowers of the ubiquitous *C.* 'Nelly Moser' retain their colour much better out of the glare of sun, although it is perhaps better on an east wall if there is a choice. One of my favourite spring-flowering clematis, *C. macropetala*, is very comfortable in the lee of a north wall, too. Try *C. m.* 'Snowbird', which is white. The lovely climbing rose 'Madame Alfred Carrière' does well on a north wall as do the burgundy red climber, 'Souvenir du Docteur Jamain', and the evergreen rambling rose 'Albéric Barbier', which has a mass of small ivory flowers.

Ivy will grow in deep shade and the evergreen climbing *Hydrangea petiolaris* is slow to establish but loves a shady wall or fence, and with its billowing white flowers has real presence.

An east-facing wall is both shady and cold, and also exposed to bright morning sunshine – which can result in frost-burn for any emerging flowers in spring. For this reason, you should never plant

« Tying in *Clematis* 'Polish Spirit' to a wigwam

camellias against an east wall. However most early clematis, such as the various *C. montana*, *C. alpina* or *C. macropetala*, are very happy on an east wall as will be all honeysuckles and many roses. Flowering quinces make ideal wall shrubs for an east-facing surface and although most fruit trees need heat for the fruit to ripen, a wall facing east is perfect for fan-training morello cherries.

Almost all climbing roses love a west-facing wall, as do all honeysuckles

Finally, a west-facing wall is ideal in almost every respect. By the time the sun has moved round to the west, the light is carrying much more heat so that a west-facing wall will be much warmer than one facing east, and the light will be much thicker and more intense. Strong colours seem to absorb this quality and reflect it so that oranges, purples and deep crimsons always look best when facing west. So, the late-summer clematis, like *C. viticella* or *C.* 'Jackmanii', are ideal, with their range of purple and plum colours.

Almost all climbing roses love a west-facing wall, as do all honeysuckles. Camellias fare well and all fruit will ripen well. Sweet peas can do very well against a west wall but it is a mistake to plant them facing south as this will be too hot and dry.

Planting and supporting

All climbers should be planted well away – at least half a yard – from any wall or fence. This might look very odd initially, but if angled back to the wall with a cane, they will soon start to grow vertically and the roots will both have more room to grow and be less likely to dry out.

Fix good strong supports for climbers before planting. Roses, wisteria and fruit do best attached to horizontal wires. Use a 12- or 14-gauge galvanised wire and attach it to screw eyes that are at least 1in clear of the fence or wall. This makes it easier to tie in the growth and also allows some ventilation. You will need a horizontal wire every

18–24in. Tensioners will take up the slack of the wire.

Clematis and honeysuckle are best supported against a wall or fence by a trellis. This can either be freestanding (but be sure to support it with really strong posts as the wind can catch it like a sail) or screwed to the surface. Like wire supports, be sure that the trellis is not flush with the wall but mounted on blocks so there is room to get your hand behind and tie in growth as needed.

I like growing clematis – especially the late-flowering varieties that are pruned hard every spring – and sweet peas up bean sticks, making wigwams from four or six good, strong sticks pushed into the ground and secured with string. These can be replaced as needed at pruning time without disturbing the plant.

Flowering Shrubs

Plant shrubs as you would a tree, in a wide hole with a loosened, but not deeply dug, base. Do not add organic material to the planting hole unless the soil is very heavy, in which case some garden compost and horticultural grit or sharp sand will help open the soil out for the initial root growth.

Always mulch thickly and widely with good compost after planting. And always water in very well, even on a wet winter's day. Allow plenty of space for your young shrubs to grow – you can always infill with temporary planting of bulbs, annuals or grasses if it looks too empty.

Remember that pruning provokes growth, so if you have a lopsided shrub, prune the weaker side back hard and leave the well-developed side alone. This will balance the shrub out.

Shrubs are not glamorous in the way that spring bulbs, a hawthorn hedge or irises are glamorous. Too much wood and straggle in their non-flowering months. But most importantly, they provide the essential middle layer that both fills and connects the space between low-growing flowers and trees.

Few gardens can exist without flowering shrubs. No other type of plant gives the same range of width or graceful spread in relationship to its height, and its woody structure means that its flowers and foliage are held more or less in space without needing support.

Shrubs are tough. Many resist cold, wind, rabbits and human neglect. Many respond gratefully to a modicum of care in the shape of a little pruning and weeding. They take very little from the gardener and give an awful lot back. Shrubberies may have a dank and gloomy Victorian image but there is no practical reason why they cannot brighten and enrich your garden throughout the year – and for many years to come.

The layered blossom of *Viburnum plicatum* f. *tomentosum* 'Mariesii' »

Shrubs for shade: The bamboos, camellia, *Choisya ternata*, *Daphne laureola pontica*, eleagnus, fatsia, *Garrya elliptica*, hypericum, *Kerria japonica*, mahonia, *Osmanthus decorus*, pyracantha, *Ribes alpinum*, skimmia, *Viburnum davidii*

Shrubs with scented flowers: Buddleia, *Ceanothus* x *delileanus* 'Gloire de Versailles', *Choisya ternata*, corylopsis, daphne, eleagnus, *Hamamelis mollis*, honeysuckle, lilac, magnolia, osmanthus, roses, viburnum

Shrubs for winter flowers: *Chimonanthus praecox* (wintersweet), *Daphne mezereum* var. *autumnalis*, *Garrya elliptica*, *Lonicera fragrantissima*, *Mahonia japonica*, *Stachyurus praecox*, *Viburnum* x *bodnantense*, *V. farreri*, *V. tinus*, winter jasmine, witch hazel

Shrubs for small gardens that can be regularly pruned back hard: Buddleia, all dogwoods, elder, hardy fuchsias, hazel, *Rubus cockburnianus*, sambucus, *Salix daphnoides*, weigela

Shrubs with purple foliage: *Acer palmatum* 'Dissectum Atropurpureum', *Cercis canadensis* 'Forest Pansy', *Corylus maxima* 'Purpurea', *Cotinus coggygria* 'Royal Purple', *Malus* x purpurea 'Lemoinei', *Rosa rubrifolia*, *Sambucus nigra* 'Guincho Purple', *Weigela florida* 'Foliis Purpureis'

Shrubs for lime soil: Berberis, brachyglottis, box, cistus, cotoneaster, daphne, deutzia, eleagnus, escallonia, euonymus, forsythia, fuchsia, hebe, kerria, kolkwitzia, mahonia, osmanthus, peony, philadelphus, potentilla, pyracantha, ribes, romneya, rosemary, rubus, lilac, viburnum, weigela

Shrubs for acidic soil: Azalea, calluna, camellia, clethra, heathers, gaultheria, *Hydrangea macrophylla*, kalmia, pernettya, pieris, rhododendrons

Lawns

I know that some people (mostly men, it has to be said) are concerned that their lawns should be as near to perfect as possible and any weed is seen as an affront to their manhood, but this has always struck me as a matter of supreme unimportance. All I am after is an even-ish area of green dominated by grass, and a few daisies, clover, dandelions, bents or moss do not trouble me too much.

But a lawn is intended to be a mown area of grass. The nature of grass is that it tends to dominate all other plants if it is regularly cut so the fact that lawns are, by definition, closely shorn, means that they are usually more or less grassy.

When it comes to mowing the lawn, the most harm that you can do is to cut it too short. The healthiest height for grass is about an inch – much longer than most people regularly mow down to. Also, do not take too much off in one go, especially in spring. A light trim will make a dramatic difference – and be much quicker than a less frequent scalping.

Making a lawn

Lawns thrive on deep, well-drained soil, so the most important thing of all is to dig the ground well and deeply, breaking up any compaction. Good drainage is the key to good grass. Adding as much sand or grit as you can manage before sowing or turfing will do more good than anything else.

The surface of your lawn will exactly replicate the surface of the soil beneath it, so rake it very carefully as even thick turf tends to accentuate any dips or hollows rather than hide them. Then tread over the raked area with your heels to flatten any soft dips and rake it again.

If you are growing grass from seed, you must decide between a) a perfect lawn or b) hard wear and tear. The two are pretty incompatible.

117

A hard-wearing lawn, suitable for family rough and tumble and more casual use will be based upon ryegrass but the perfect sward you find on bowling or golf greens will be mainly Chewings fescue. This creates a finer, more velvety surface and can tolerate being cut very short indeed – but is not at all hard-wearing.

Shady soil needs a special mix of seed. If in doubt, ryegrass mixes are much cheaper than grass for fine lawns and price is likely to be as accurate an indicator of what you are buying as anything else.

When you buy turf it should be moist, green, reasonably thin and weed-free. Long rolls are better than short slabs of turf because they dry out more slowly. Try and get it delivered the same day as you will lay it, but if you have it delivered more than 48 hours before you can use it, unroll the turf on any surface and water it well.

The secret of establishing a good lawn is sun, moisture and good drainage. Provide those three things and the grass is guaranteed to thrive, and where grass thrives, almost all else will play second fiddle, including moss, daisies, thistles, bents, buttercups and dandelions.

The secret of establishing a good lawn is sun, moisture and good drainage

The quantity of sun cannot be controlled but you can cut back overhanging branches and most of the time there is enough rain to provide the moisture. I would never water any established lawn in the UK as they all recover from seemingly disastrous drought. Grass is very tough. However, drainage is the hardest aspect of care to maintain because the very act of walking on a lawn – let alone riding bikes or playing football or whatever – will compact the soil. This is why it is a good idea to aerate the turf each autumn and spring, and to brush in sand if the soil is heavy.

Sometimes the simplicity of mown grass and clipped hedges is all you need »

Lawn problems

1. **Worms** are a sign of a healthy soil; their casts can be brushed back into the ground to enrich it. They are a nuisance and unsightly for a few weeks in autumn but do no long-term harm.

2. **Ants** are becoming increasingly common, creating powdery fine little casts, but again do no real harm. Just brush them back into the grass.

3. **'Fairy rings'** and pale brown toadstools are caused by the fungus *Marasmius oreades*. Typically, there will be a stimulation of grass growth at the periphery of the infection, causing the grass to turn dark green. The usual cause is something rotting under your lawn such as an old tree stump or root.

4. **Leatherjackets** are the grubs of crane flies. They eat grass roots, causing dead patches. The simplest way of dealing with them is to aerate your lawn well to prevent stagnant soil conditions.

5. **Red thread disease** causes patches of grass to become bleached; the red growths of the disease appear between the bleached grass.

6. **Chafer grubs** eat grass roots causing patches to turn brown and die. Encourage plenty of birds into the garden that will be happy to eat them for you. Pull away infected grass and re-seed or turf.

Weeds

Want to know which are the most successful plants in my garden? The ones that grow lustily every year, whatever the weather? Almost certainly the same ones that are thriving best in your garden too, namely weeds. A weed is a plant hero, an adaptor and a survivor, coping with any weather and outperforming all plants around it.

Some plants did not start out as weeds but were introduced as garden treasures. The most famous of these is Japanese knotweed, introduced in 1825, now officially Britain's most problematic weed and illegal to plant.

Some simply become weeds in a particular garden because they do so well. Anything that self-seeds runs the risk of that designation, as do perennials that creep out sideways like the *Lysimachia ciliata* 'Firecracker' in our Jewel Garden or the shuttlecock fern that is now swamping my Damp Garden, both of which plants started out as carefully nurtured treasures.

But do not despise weeds. They are the best adapted, most successful plants in your garden and are expert at making the most of your soil. Study what weeds you have and where they are growing, and you will learn a lot about the plants that are likely to do best in your garden.

1. **A** rash of docks, mare's-tail, ox-eye daisies, creeping buttercup and rushes says you have a poorly drained, heavy soil.
2. **Chicory**, bindweed, silverweed and greater plantain are a sure sign of compaction.
3. **If** your soil is acidic, then you will host dandelions, stinging nettles and sorrel.
4. **Salad** burnet, campion, charlock, poppies and nodding thistle indicate an alkaline or limey soil with a pH above 7.
5. **Nettles** are also always a sign of high levels of phosphate and nitrogen, and will always grow in damp areas where animals and humans have congregated.

6. **Daisies**, wild carrot and mullein grow on ground low in fertility.
7. **You** should celebrate if you find your garden overcome with chickweed, henbit or pigweed because they are a sign of rich, fertile soil.

However you arrive at it, weeds are there in every garden and take up an awful lot of a gardener's time and energy. Yet many are beautiful. Dandelions, buttercups, ground elder and daisies all have lovely flowers, especially en masse (which, alas, they so often are). All are the ideal plant for the soil and situation if not for our carefully constructed scheme of things.

The good news

The good news is that the more weeds you have the healthier and better conditioned is your soil. Secondly, the greater the diversity of weed types, the greater the range of chosen plants that you will eventually be able to grow. A wide range of weeds will also attract a wide selection of insects and do much to contribute to the holistic balance of your garden – which is the very essence of successful organic gardening.

Weeds can also make a good green manure. Cut the flowers off before they set seed, use the top growth for the compost heap, and dig in the roots for a mass of organic material to enrich the soil structure.

Some modern weeds have been cultivated for their edibility. Many people eat young nettles in spring as a vegetable (like spinach) or as a soup. I personally find them delicious and they are exceptionally rich in iron. And in the past, ground elder, chickweed and fat hen have all been gathered and even cultivated as vegetables. Who knows what prize veg will be rampant weeds in a few hundred years' time?

Weeds are not only good for wildlife but
can also look as good as a manicured border »

Dealing with weeds

I am an organic gardener and do not use chemicals of any sort – so will not advocate herbicides. But whatever ideology you may have about chemical use, my experience is that most weeds are controllable without them. It goes without saying that prevention is always better than cure.

Firstly, always check plants that you buy or are given, especially woody plants that can easily host the roots of ground elder, bindweed or couch grass.

The second thing is to avoid the situation getting bad – or at least any worse. Tackle weeds as and when you notice them. In practice this means that it is a constant job. But I use it as a chance to get close to my plants and to judge the state of the soil, as well as being part of keeping the place looking beautiful. So do not see weeding as a terrible burden imposed upon you but enjoy it as part of real gardening.

Chemicals are very good at destroying weeds but they can also destroy plants you want to keep, let alone the micro-diversity of your soil and the insect life of your garden. Weedkillers are pushed hard by chemical companies because they are enormously profitable and often effective in the short term. But in the medium to long term, they are actively harmful to your whole ecosystem and that is not good gardening. We are here to look after and nurture this lovely earth, not blast everything that momentarily stands in our way.

There is another approach. Manage weeds so that you control them rather than they controlling you. Here is how.

1. **Timing:** You must remove weeds before they seed. The old adage, 'one year's seeding means seven years' weeding' is pretty much accurate. If you cannot dig them up, then cut the tops off – using a mower if need be – until such a time as you can get at them properly.
2. **Hoe:** If you grow vegetables, a hoe is essential for removing weeds. The secret of hoeing is to do it little and often. Always hoe on a dry day, preferably in the morning so that the weeds will wilt and die in the sun (they can and will often regrow in the wet). The secret of hoeing is to keep the blade sharp and run it lightly under the

surface of the soil in a push/pull action rather than jabbing at individual weeds. If you have a very weed-infested bit of ground you want to cultivate – and remember, weed-infestation implies good healthy soil – and the weeds have not yet gone to seed, then a good tip is to hoe the weeds off with a mattock or large draw hoe, rake up what you can and compost it, then dig the whole area over. This will not get rid of the perennial weeds but will allow you to grow a crop of fast-growing and weed-suppressing vegetables like potatoes, beans or squashes, or sow a green manure.

3. **Hand-weed:** A hoe is often too crude a weapon for a border. The answer is to get down on your knees and carefully remove every scrap of weed with your fingers and a hand fork. I love it. You really get to know your soil and your plants, and the seedlings and herbaceous perennials coming through, and you improve an area dramatically without major disruption.

4. **Roots:** The best way to remove all perennial weeds is to dig up their roots. With nettles or brambles, this is actually quite easy. But bindweed, ground elder and couch grass will regrow from the tiniest scrap of root and as these are very brittle, it is easy to break off a piece and leave it in the ground. Do not be discouraged. We all miss bits of root. Just go back if you notice regrowth and take some more out. In time, you will get on top of it, as well as dramatically weakening it and reducing the spread.

5. **Mulch:** Cover every piece of bare soil with a light-excluding but moisture-permeable layer. Garden compost is best of all but anything will do. Well-rotted horse or cattle manure is good but cattle manure can include a lot of weed seeds if it is not sufficiently rotted.

If you are using an organic mulch (i.e. one that will rot down into the soil) spread it at least 2in thick. This will not stop existing perennial weeds growing through but will make them much easier to pull up. And although it will not eradicate perennials, it will certainly weaken them. This is important since if some weeds are allowed to get healthy and strong, their spread is phenomenal. Bindweed can cover 30 square yards in one season and one creeping buttercup plant will colonise five square yards in a year.

The most effective mulches cut out all light and water from the weeds, starving their growth. Black polythene with a 400–600 gauge will certainly do this. However, as well as looking horrible, it also destroys all other growth so is only useful for clearing ground prior to planting. A woven plastic 'landscape fabric' is a better long-term bet as it allows moisture through, but it doesn't look much better. When I use these I always cover them with a layer of chipped bark.

But on a border, a loose mulch of organic material is needed. Anything will make a difference but for pure weed control, heavy-duty bark chippings are excellent. Personally, I prefer garden compost, mushroom compost, gravel or cardboard covered with grass clippings.

For pure weed control, heavy-duty bark chippings are excellent

The advantages of these organic mulches is that they also feed the soil and improve its structure, so whilst they inhibit weeds, they also promote the growth of the plants that you value. But whatever you use must be in a thick layer to be effective. Minimum two inches, and ideally twice that or even more. It is always better to mulch a small area well than to try and spread it thinly and widely.

If all else fails, it is worth constantly cutting back the growth of perennial weeds. This will weaken them and at the very least limit their spread. Often, especially for bracken and ground elder, this is the only feasible action and it does help.

I use a flame gun for our paths and this is very effective. It needs doing about once a month. However, you do have to be careful not to damage adjoining plants through heat radiation.

Here is a list of my own worst weeds.
Very difficult perennial weeds (require long-term strategy or inspired acceptance): Horsetail, Japanese knotweed, lesser celandine

Perennial weeds to take very seriously (dig up every scrap of root and burn): Bindweed, couch grass, creeping buttercup, ground elder

Perennial weeds to work at (dig up as and when you can): Broad-leafed dock, burdock, creeping thistle, nettles, spear thistle

Perennial weeds that are handsome but intrusive: Comfrey, daisy, dandelion, deadnettle, feverfew, greater celandine, alkanet, hogweed, mallow, plantain, rosebay willowherb, selfheal, silverweed, teasel

Annual weeds (never let them seed!): Caper spurge, chickweed, fat hen, goosegrass, groundsel, Himalayan balsam, knotgrass, petty spurge, prickly sowthistle, shepherd's needle, shepherd's purse

Finally, do not try and eradicate all weeds from the garden. This will not only save you a lot of time and energy but will also greatly enhance the wildlife that feed off them in one form or other. A clump of nettles or the odd thistle, dandelion or ramble of chickweed here and there does more good than harm.

Fungus

'Fairy rings' on lawns always provoke a flurry of anxious letters and emails. What on earth can one do about this recurring blight of overlush, coarse green grass on an otherwise immaculate green sward? How can the toadstools that pop up in that grass be eliminated?

By the same token I can guarantee a batch of anxious requests, usually in autumn, about how to deal with the horrors of honey fungus or, more often, about the anxieties of not spotting honey fungus in time to save a favourite tree or shrub.

In my own garden, box blight has ravaged growth on hundreds of yards of hedges and destroyed over 60 large topiary balls, some of which I have been training and nurturing for over 30 years. This year I cut down four Portuguese laurels because they had silver leaf, a fungal infection that lifts the surface of the leaves and eventually kills the tree.

All these are fungal problems. All have got worse over the past ten years and are set to continue getting worse for the foreseeable future.

Yet I can honestly say that I welcome fungi in my garden and acknowledge that without it, very little indeed would grow. In just a teaspoonful of soil, you would expect to find around 10,000 species of fungi. These are part of the indescribably complex synthesis that enables plants to grow healthily.

Most fungi exist below the ground as mycelium, which have widespreading filaments that feed on decomposing matter. So a 'fairy ring' in your lawn marks the extent of the mycelium growing outwards underground like the spokes of a bicycle wheel. The reason that the grass is greener and longer at the outer limit of the circle is that the fungus has used all the nutrients in the soil within the circle, whereas at the edge, it excretes chemicals into the ground ahead to provide it with food, and the grass temporarily responds by growing lusher. When the fungus meets a barrier of some kind it will stop and die, and the grass within it will recover its health. As to stopping or limiting it, nothing is more effective than reducing compaction and providing good drainage.

Most fungi thrive in warm, damp conditions and our mild autumns and winters, and damp summers are making fungal 'problems' more common. The truth is that every garden will suffer from fungal problems all the time. But good housekeeping can help a great deal.

Light and air should be encouraged within borders and among individual plants. Black spot on roses always thrives in warm, damp conditions. Canker and scab in fruit trees flourish where the drainage around the fruit tree's roots is poor and where unpruned branches restrict airflow.

I welcome fungi in my garden and acknowledge that without it, very little indeed would grow

Clematis wilt is caused by the fungus *Phoma clematidina* entering into a damaged part of the stem. The best defence is to plant deeply with at least an inch of stem below soil level, and to carefully support growing stems so that they do not get damaged by wind.

Honey fungus, *Armillaria*, manifests itself above ground by clumps of tawny toadstools appearing from early autumn at the base of trees or bushes. These toadstools are perfectly harmless but between the bark and wood you will find white mats of mycelium, and around affected roots, just below the soil surface, you will find black, lace-like strands called rhizomorphs. It is these that spread the fungus from dead to neighbouring living, woody tissue.

But life depends upon fungi. Every compost heap needs fungi to turn woody waste material like plant stems into crumbly compost. And all dead wood is decomposed primarily by fungal action. So dousing your soil with fungicide is like dropping an atom bomb to kill an individual. It is rarely worth the collateral damage to your garden. Instead, give thanks to the fungi that enable our gardens to grow.

Pests

The best defence against any pest or disease is a healthy plant. Plants that grow in a soil with good structure, that are not in any way forced against the weather, location or in their growth, are in my experience remarkably trouble-free.

The second important defence against inevitable so-called 'pests' in the garden is to encourage and sustain a balanced ecosystem. Leave your garden untouched, and a balance will establish itself containing a vast range of creatures that live with the plants.

But by definition, a garden is an unnatural place. One of the skills is to assimilate that tight human control into a balance with the local wildlife. At first, when you 'go organic' and deliberately stop using all herbicides, pesticides and fungicides, there will be a degree of anarchy. Certain pests will dominate. Certain fungal problems or diseases will get worse. Stick with it. You have created an imbalance in your garden and nature is restoring sanity but this involves a certain amount of see-sawing.

Expect everything to get worse for the first year and then start to improve thereafter. It takes about three years for there to be a relaxed, self-sustaining equilibrium between plants, pests and predators but once established, it is very easy to maintain.

Make the garden a comfortable, easy place for your plants to thrive in rather than a collection of trophies clinging onto life despite rather than because of the soil, climate and position. The best advice for any gardener is always to work with nature wherever you are, however, certain creatures do present more problems than others.

Moles

Mole numbers are on the increase, possibly due to wet and mild winters extending the breeding season. Moles can move their own weight in soil every minute and they produce a network of tunnels mostly about 2ft beneath the soil surface. The result is earthy carnage to a lawn. However, there are two consolations if your garden is occupied by moles. The first is that it is an indicator that you have a healthy soil with plenty of earthworms – which are their favourite food, although they also eat slugs. The second is that you will be provided with a good supply of molehills which, mixed with garden compost and sharp sand, make excellent potting compost.

Moles are solitary, only meeting up in the breeding season, which is between the end of February and May. Then they will make long tunnels just below the surface of the soil when looking for a mate. Although it is sometimes hard to believe, it is very unlikely that anything other than the largest garden will contain more than two moles, as their average density is about four per acre.

Rabbits

For anyone who lives in a remotely rural position, these can be a real pest. I wrap fine chicken wire around all my fruit trees because they can easily kill a tree simply by nibbling round the trunk. If rabbits are a major problem, the only solution is to put up a chicken-wire fence round as big an area as you can, sinking it a foot deep into the ground and at least 3ft high. This is expensive and a pain to do, but will make a rabbit-free zone in which to grow the plants that matter to you most. Remember that any enclosure is only as secure as its gate. Rabbits seem not to eat certain plants including hostas, foxgloves, crocosmias, euphorbias, geraniums, irises, kniphofia, peonies and nepeta.

Slugs and snails

The healthy plant syndrome applies to slugs and snails as much as any pest, and since there are a number of slug and snail predators, from birds, hedgehogs, toads and moles to beetles, let that predatory balance establish itself.

One useful tip is to grow fairly large batches of lettuce in blocks.

This literally saturates the slug larder. The lettuces grow faster than the slugs can eat them, provided that they are grown initially in a slug-free zone like a cold frame or greenhouse and are planted out when they are growing strongly.

The biggest slugs do not necessarily do the most damage. There are four main garden slugs:

1. **The grey field slug**, which will eat anything and will reproduce three generations a year.
2. **The garden slug** is shiny black with an orange belly, and is also omnivorous; its party trick is to eat off bean plants at ground level and riddle potatoes with holes.
3. **The keeled slug** is black, with a thin orange line down the centre of its back; it spends almost all its life underground, feeding off root crops but will also eat what it can when it surfaces.
4. **The black slug** can come in almost any colour but is differentiated from all others by its size, which can reach 8in long. Although this monster looks as though it will eat you out of garden and home, in fact it is the least harmful of all garden slugs.

Rotovate to get at the keeled slugs and handpick the field and garden slugs. Leave the poor black slug alone.

Caterpillars

The only caterpillar that really wreaks havoc in my garden is the cabbage white. There are actually two types: the large and the small white. The large white butterfly lays its eggs on the leaves of any brassicas (cabbages, turnips, radishes) and the emerging yellow and black caterpillars cover them by the hundred, stripping the young plants to a skeleton. The butterflies are attracted by the mustard in brassicas, which the plants develop as a defence against insects. The butterflies take on the mustard taste in their own tissues, which works effectively against predation by birds.

The small white lays deeper into the plant and has pure green

Cabbage white butterfly caterpillars feasting on a cauliflower leaf »

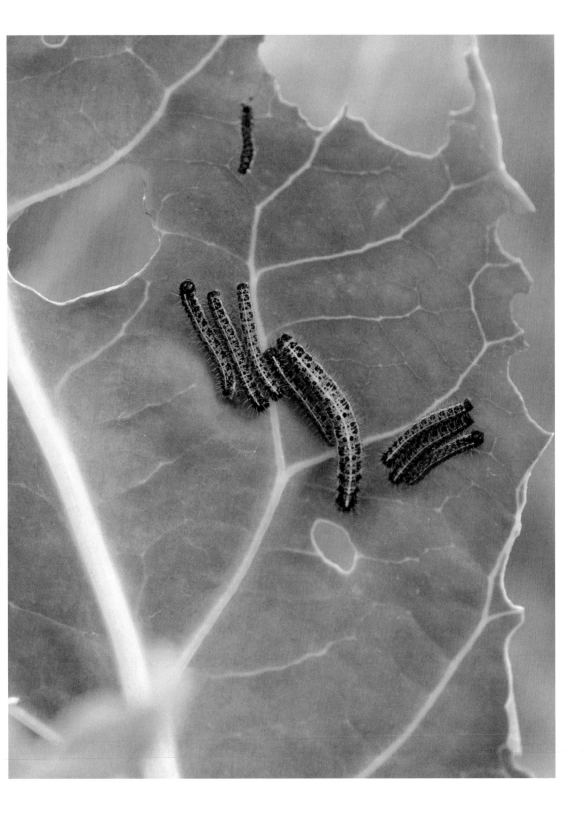

caterpillars, which do their work less conspicuously but to just as noxious an effect. Spraying the plants with salt water can help, but the best cure is prevention, covering the plants with a fine net from the minute they are planted until October. Otherwise you must go through each plant every day, picking off the caterpillars by hand.

Aphids

The best action that the gardener can take against aphids is to encourage ladybirds, hoverflies and lacewings into the garden by planting plenty of umbellifers like dill and fennel, or by letting a patch of carrots go to seed. Tits eat a huge amount of aphids as will parasitic wasps. But again, one comes back to the need for healthy plants that do not have too much lush, soft growth, as that is meat and drink to all aphids.

The lettuce-root aphid thrives in late summer in very dry conditions. Lettuce will wilt a little and then suddenly completely collapse because the aphids feed off the roots. Lift all the affected plants and compost them, and do not replant with lettuce for another year. The best prevention is to keep your lettuces well-watered.

Vine weevils

These are second only to slugs and snails as a horticultural hate figure, particularly to plants in containers, yet I confess that I have never had to deal with them in any garden of my own. They are recognisable either from the beetle-like adult covered with yellow specks or the larvae, which are 'c'-shaped and creamy white. The adult will eat characteristic irregular holes around the edges of leaves but it is the larvae that do the real damage. The adults are almost all female and will each lay over a hundred eggs in the soil around the host plant from late July. The larvae will then feed on the host's roots until the following spring, when they pupate.

There are pathogenic nematodes that can be watered into the pots at this time of year, and which will attack the grubs. To work properly, the compost must be warm and moist, so water the plants first. The best way to deal with adults is to look for them with a torch at night and pick them off, and before buying any plant in a container, take it out of the pot and check carefully for adults in spring and larvae in late summer.

Pigeons

Pigeons will strip cabbages, lettuces and peas to a stub unless preventative action is taken. As with caterpillars, prevention is the best answer. If pigeons are really bad in your area, then some kind of permanent netting or cage that can be placed over young plants is a good investment. A temporary net can be made from canes supporting upturned pots, with light netting draped over these, but be sure that there is plenty of clearance between the netting and the plants because the birds will land on the net and peck through it if they can.

Failing installing protective netting, some hanging, glittery material that catches in the wind is very effective. We used to use milk bottle tops threaded on string in the days when there were such things, but nowadays old CDs or strips of silver foil will do the trick.

Woodlice

I have a very soft spot for woodlice. They are the only species of crustacean on this planet that inhabits dry land as opposed to watery places. They feed off decaying wood and are an important cog in the eco-machine that recycles decaying vegetation. However, they can occasionally nibble seedlings in a greenhouse, where the warm damp attracts them. But they much prefer decaying wood and leaves so the best defence is to keep the greenhouse tidy and the plants moving.

But the critical thing is that they do far more good for the gardener than harm and in any event they have a range of predators such as toads, centipedes, spiders, millipedes and wasps that will attack and devour them – hence their defensive strategy of forming a tight little armoured ball until danger passes.

Voles

Voles can be a severe, if usually unseen, problem. These small mice-like rodents live largely under and in tussocky grass but will eat bulbs, roots, seeds and flower buds, as well as gnawing bark, and can cause real damage without ever being visible to the average gardener. The short-tailed field vole tends to go in for lemming-like population explosions, causes huge damage, then eats itself out of house and home and provides easy meat for the local owl population. Nothing you can do except be stoical and pleased for the boost in owl numbers.

Rats

Rats do surprisingly little harm short of terrifying and horrifying gardeners. According to our local rat catcher (whose business is rather ominously expanding hugely), sheds and compost heaps are the two places where you are likely to find rats. The answer is to raise your shed a foot off the ground and then buy a terrier that can get under there and sort the rats out. Works a treat. As for compost heaps, I have only ever seen a rat in ours once in the past 20 years. The secret is to chop all composting material up, turn the heap often so it is hot, and never add meat, fats or any cooked material. The result is too hot and unpalatable for rats to take up permanent lodgings.

Squirrels

When I first moved to this garden, there was just one tree which was a very old and rather gnarled hazel. This bore a quantity of nuts every year, although most would be snaffled by squirrels before they were ripe enough to be gathered and eaten by us. But after a year or two I noticed hazel seedlings popping up, which were nuts that the squirrels had gathered and buried and then forgotten about. These had then germinated and become little hazel saplings.

So I started to dig them up and pot them. After a few years, I had about a hundred of them, so decided to plant a little wood or hazel coppice. Now, 20 odd years later, this little wood provides us with all our bean sticks, lots of nuts, and is a beautiful part of the garden, filled with spring flowers like primroses, anemones and bluebells. I suppose I should thank the squirrels for this although it is hard to find a gardener – and especially a forester – to say a good word for them, or at least for the grey squirrel.

This was introduced into this country from its native North America at the end of the nineteenth century, when ten were released at Woburn Abbey in 1890. They were first considered charming novelties but it soon became apparent that wherever the grey squirrel took residence, the red was quickly driven out or killed. This was primarily because the greys will eat a wide range of nuts and seeds – as well as eggs and young chicks in spring – whereas the red will only eat smaller seeds such as pine and spruce nuts.

Now grey squirrels are everywhere and do huge damage to forestry – and garden trees – by gnawing the bark of trees. All a tree's food and water is carried from the roots to the branches and leaves via the thin cambium layer that lies between the bark and the wood. Any creature that gnaws a ring around the trunk will cut this supply line and kill the tree.

Wasps

It is hard to find many good words to say about wasps. Bees sting as a last resort and invariably kill themselves in the process, but wasps will attack seemingly unprovoked and sting repeatedly. Bumblebees are loveable and honeybees noble – but wasps? Wasps are just scary.

Bumblebees are loveable and honeybees noble – but wasps? Wasps are just scary

But good. For a start, there are lots of different kinds of wasps to be found in every garden. Britain has eight kinds of social wasps that share nests and these include the hornet. But there are another

230 species of non-social kinds that live almost solitary lives. They have many guises and lifestyles but most are digger wasps that all have hammer heads and very narrow waists (hence the 'wasp-like waist'). They excavate holes in dry banks, which they provision with live prey – usually caterpillars and aphids but also flies and beetles, and even bees.

But it is the social wasps that dominate gardens towards the end of summer. They build exquisitely beautiful nests made from chewed wood pulp that are as light as a feather but strong enough to house thousands of wasps and their eggs. Each one of these delicate, complex constructions is a little wasp township and a miracle of ingenuity.

The most often asked question is: what use are wasps? What are they for? You might well ask the same for humans but in general, they are carnivores that eat a large number of caterpillars and aphids. It is only in late summer that they develop their sweet tooth and that time coincides with a huge glut of worker wasps that have finished their nest-building duties and are thus free to hunt for sugar in any form. And as well as predating on garden pests, wasps themselves provide a tasty treat for badgers, buzzards and, above all, spiders which are, perhaps surprisingly, their biggest and most deadly enemy.

Earwigs

In late summer it is very common to find that the petals of dahlias are clearly chewed and nibbled, often reduced to tattered rags and pale imitations of their supposed glory. The culprits are earwigs that have a distinct penchant for what is – to them at least – a juicy and delicious dahlia flower.

Conventional horticultural advice is to trap the earwigs overnight by placing an upturned pot or a matchbox on a cane by the dahlia and stuffing it with straw. The earwig goes into this at dawn to rest up, thinking it a convenient safe haven before realising that you, the gardener, are about to come along and extract it from its strawy bed before doing something very unpleasant and probably terminal.

But the common earwig is a fascinating creature. Earwigs certainly do not rely upon the dahlia for their daily diet, being pretty much omnivorous and eating other insects that gardeners consider as pests. They thrive in mild, damp conditions, which makes the UK almost ideal for them, but can most readily be found under loose bark or in any woody crevice in great clusters – attracted to each other by the scent pheromones that they release. The females lay about 30 cream-coloured eggs in underground nests in the new year, and the nymphs hatch out in April, then go through a number of cycles, during which time the female will protect and feed the young until they are large enough to foray out on their own.

They seem to like dahlias because in late summer and autumn – when dahlias are at their best – the massed petals of the flower heads provide ideal shelter for them and, once ensconced, they nibble a little at their surroundings.

Common earwigs have wings and are able to fly but rarely do, whereas there are three other native species of earwig that fly much more often and I – or more accurately the lamp by my bedside – have been buzzed by earwigs as I read in bed.

One way of telling the difference between the sexes is that males have curved pincers whereas those of the female are more or less straight.

Compost

The best that you can do for soil – and therefore for your plants and entire garden – is to make good garden compost, including as much material grown in your own soil as possible.

Compost is like a starter dough. Its most useful role is to top up the soil's existing bacterial and fungal levels, and encourage the right conditions for plants to access the soil's nutrients. Its role as a soil conditioner is an excellent side effect – but one that can also be achieved through using manure or any other organic material. But only garden compost has the richness and diversity of micro-organisms.

Organic material does not 'rot' in the soil but is broken down largely by digestion, most notably by earthworms, bacteria and fungi, although scores of invertebrates, insects and nematodes – as well as slugs and snails – also contribute to the process. Each of the uncountable organisms that live in the soil – and it is reckoned that there are billions in every pinch – take nourishment from the organic matter and move on, so that by the time the organic matter is accessible by plant roots, it has been through a lengthy and – as yet – unknowably complex digestion process.

Compost is like a starter dough. Its most useful role is to top up the soil's existing bacterial and fungal levels

In light of this complexity, isolating any perceived particular 'pest' or 'problem' is like threading a needle with a bulldozer and will almost certainly harm the ecosystem and structure of your soil. And that harms your garden.

When organic material has been completely broken down, what is left in the soil is humus – and humus is broadly speaking soil that has a high content of long-lasting organic material. Soil of any type that is rich in humus will only need an inch or so of compost added every year as a mulch to provide good growing conditions.

....

Making compost

Compost is made from a combination of 'green' material, high in nitrogen – such as fresh grass clippings or vegetable waste – and 'brown' matter, high in carbon – such as straw, dried plant stems and cardboard.

Pure 'green' material will decompose very quickly but can turn into a slimy sludge. Pure 'brown' material will take much longer to rot down but will end up in a more manageable state.

The ratio of green to brown will vary according to time of year and place, but it is best when it is somewhere between 20–30 parts carbon to 1 part nitrogen. Fresh clippings from a lawn are about the 'greenest' matter a garden can regularly provide and these are about 50:50 nitrogen to carbon, so a good rule of thumb is to have at least twice the volume of brown material, high in carbon, to the volume of soft, green material, rich in nitrogen. To that end, it is a good idea to have a supply of straw, bracken, dried stems or cardboard to hand.

Making good compost is very straightforward. There are two ways: one fast and laborious, the other slow and easy. For either method, you must gather all the organic material from your home and garden – meaning kitchen waste (but not meat, fats or cooked starches, as these will attract vermin faster than they will be composted), grass, any and all plant material, green prunings such as summer hedge clippings, cardboard, shredded paper and any animal manure that you have access to.

In my garden we use the fast, laborious method. We pile all the organic material up in a collecting bay and then once a week take it out and mow or shred it before adding it to the first compost bay. A reasonably powerful mower does this job very well and dramatically speeds up the composting process.

When the first compost bay is full, we transfer its contents to a second compost bay, which stimulates further composting, and we gradually refill the first compost bay from the collecting bay.

We then, ideally, turn the contents of the second bay every two or three weeks, but once a month is also practical and effective. By the third or fourth turning – i.e. after three or four months – it will have become a sweet-smelling, crumbly, brown compost, pleasant to handle and ready for use.

Save your very best compost for growing vegetables and as a component of potting compost. The twiggy, slightly 'undercooked' batches – and we all produce them – can be used to mulch around trees, hedges and shrubs.

Save your very best compost for growing vegetables and as a component of potting compost

If you haven't the time or ability to turn your compost regularly, you can use the 'slow' method. This involves accumulating a heap – ideally long and low so it has a large surface area – of all your compostable material, and leaving it for 12–18 months to slowly decompose. After a year, the interior will have become fine compost. The exterior can then be used to start a new heap. Although easy, this method does require more space than the average garden can spare, and more time.

However you make compost, remember that the work is being done primarily by bacteria, with an important role played by fungi. For bacteria to do their work well, they need air and moisture. Turning the compost will provide the air, while moisture can be regulated either by leaving the heap open to the rain or by watering it with a hose as necessary.

All garden and kitchen waste is regularly turned from bay to bay until it comes out the other end as perfect garden compost »

Tools

Whilst there is a lot of truth in the saying 'a bad workman blames his tools', and whilst a good gardener will make a lovely garden with whatever is to hand, good-quality, well cared-for tools foster a kind of respect and sensuous pleasure that inevitably improves both the experience of gardening and the garden. Just as a chef uses high-quality knives, so a gardener should respect their work enough to use the best tools they can get hold of. You dig better with a good spade, create a finer tilth with a good rake, and prune better with sharp secateurs.

Trust hand tools and physical labour. We have forgotten how mountains can be moved by hand. Plugging away is extraordinarily effective. You do not have to use machines. Scythes cut grass very well. Axes and saws split and cut up wood. Spades and forks cultivate the soil. There is dignity and respect in the simple but expert use of an implement designed and refined to serve one purpose very well.

Mend everything. Take a pride in the longevity of your tools and implements. Value their idiosyncrasies. Learn their heft. Throwing away should always be an act of failure or a painful parting.

If you cannot make a tool yourself, find the best you can afford. Value the quality. Pay properly for this and then treasure and look after it accordingly.

The essentials

You only really need a spade, fork, rake, hoe, trowel, secateurs and a knife. Everything else is luxury – and I love the luxury of using specialist tools – but however much you enjoy using a wide range of beautiful tools, nobody needs them to make a beautiful garden.

I was visited once by a farmer from central Africa. He was tall and lean and immaculate in his suit. I showed him my garden. In particular, he was fascinated by the rows of tools in the tool shed. Very shyly he told me he farmed 5 acres from which he fed three extended families. His only tool was a mattock. When the handle broke, he had to walk half a day to find a tree to cut a new one, and then half a day back.

Every gardener must have a good spade. There are plenty of 'bad' spades out there but a good spade will hold its edge, feel light and easy to use, yet be robust enough to dig as long as your back (or in my case knees) will hold out. It will also be versatile enough to dig a hole for a large tree or divide an herbaceous plant into precise sections. A border spade should have the same virtues but is much smaller and useful for working in tight spaces.

You only really need a spade, fork, rake, hoe, trowel, secateurs and a knife

You also need a fork. I prefer square tines (as opposed to round or flat), not too long, not too curved, stainless steel and robust enough to serve arduous use. A small border fork is also useful for lifting a plant without damaging its neighbours. Digging is always best done with a spade. Keep the fork for breaking up the soil once dug, or for lifting plants.

One rake will do but three is a counsel of perfection. For general preparation of a seedbed, a round-tined flathead rake is best. A spring-tine rake doubles for scratching grass and as a leaf collector, while rubber rakes are useful for gathering up leaves from borders without damaging plants and seedlings.

If you grow vegetables you must have a hoe. The design of it depends upon whether you push the cutting edge through the soil or pull it back towards you. I think that for smaller, annual weeds it is best to push, cutting through the roots of weeds just below the surface of the soil. Keep the hoe sharp and keep it small. It is a big mistake to try and save time by using a big-bladed hoe. A small one is twice as useful because it is much more versatile.

Bigger weeds are best chopped out with a swan-neck or draw hoe.

If you find a good mattock they can be very useful for rough digging as well as weeding.

You do need a good trowel or two for planting – one big and one small. A word of caution: cheap trowels just do not last, so go for quality of manufacture and metal. The same goes for knives and for the final essential part of gardening kit – good secateurs. As with any cutting tool, secateurs are only as good as the steel that the blades are made from. The shape, colour or detail of design is a matter of subjective taste but high-quality steel holds an edge and makes pruning easy.

Secateurs should be as much part of your gardening attire as your working boots. I always carry my secateurs in a pocket and the result is that all my right-hand pockets eventually get holes in them, but that is the price I pay for wearing braces rather than a belt that would carry a tool holster.

Good tools make gardening a pleasure and last a lifetime »

Planting

Any deciduous trees and shrubs, whether in a container or bare-root, are best planted when they are dormant, between the beginning of November and the end of February.

You can often get away with planting in October and March but avoid planting any but the smallest trees or shrubs in summer unless you can water them weekly. If at all practical, it is better to wait until the following October if you miss the March deadline.

It is best to move any deciduous trees and shrubs between mid-October and mid-November. The soil still has some warmth then, which means that the roots will grow a little and get established before the new foliage appears the following spring. This means that there is less stress on the plant from the outset.

Evergreen trees and shrubs never have a true dormant season but are most vulnerable to bad weather in winter. They should be planted (or moved) in April or early May, after the soil has begun to warm but when the weather is not too hot. Alternatively, they can be planted or moved in September so the roots can establish before winter.

The thicker and woodier a root is, the less it matters when it comes to planting. It is the tiny, hair-like roots of even the biggest trees that are the most important as these are doing the feeding. So never leave a bare-root plant sitting unprotected in a cold wind while you prepare the hole. These fragile roots dry up very easily so, when planting – and especially with bare-root plants – always have a bin bag or some hessian to hand to protect them and make sure that they have had a long drink before planting.

Planting holes

Plant all trees, shrubs and hedging plants in shallow but wide holes. Conventional wisdom has been that you dig a hole deep enough to add plenty of organic material and then plant into this. It is a mistake and exposes the plant to greater wind and rain damage, as well as encouraging slower growth because the roots are slower to leave the planting hole. A tree's health is measured not by how deep the roots go but how far they spread. Dig only a spade's-depth (a 'spit') but make the radius of the hole at least twice as wide as it is deep.

Loosen the sides and bottom of the hole with a fork and plant so that the roots are on a cone or mound with the base of the trunk or stem an inch or two above ground level. Firm it very well with your foot round this cone so you are buttressing the roots rather than squashing them and backfill the rest of the soil. Stake all but the smallest trees at 45 degrees with the stake angled into the prevailing wind, tie securely and water very well. Finally mulch thickly. Keep watered for the first year and renew the mulch every year for at least five years. Remove the stake after three years.

A tree's health is measured not by how deep the roots go but how far they spread

Most of the feeding roots of trees and shrubs are in the first 12in below the surface. So if a plant is visibly ailing, the first course of action should be to weed around its base to the width of its canopy, water it and then mulch that area very well, preferably with good compost.

Always firm plants in well without crushing them. I find using my feet for trees and shrubs and hands for herbaceous plants works out fine.

When planting something grown in a pot, check the roots before putting it into the planting hole. If it is at all potbound – i.e. the roots are either a solid mass or growing sideways around the edge of the container – do not try and tease them open but gently break them with your fingers, which will stimulate regrowth out into the soil.

In the end, the healthiest plants are those that have adapted to the soil and situation that they are in. Some of this adaption is evolutionary but a surprising amount is very local and quick. Planting carefully so the roots have the best chance of getting out into the soil is an important factor in this early adaption and subsequent health.

What goes around, comes around. That means that you might as well try and get it right first time. Every action has a reaction and this really applies to the garden.

The temptations to take short cuts, to cheat a little, to try and somehow trick plants to behave quicker, bigger or for longer, are there for all of us at some time.

But in my experience, you should grow plants, taking every care with the seed, choosing – or ideally making – the seed compost with real thought, pricking out the seedlings at the best moment and with full attention, growing them on, checking every day, observing and reacting to what is actually happening rather than what should or could happen – or even to what has happened a thousand times before – then either pot them on or plant them out at the most propitious moment, bearing in mind the weather, soil, season, and every stage of the plants' future life. If you do all these things as consciously as possible, then the chances are extremely high that the plants will grow healthily and well with minimal further assistance from you.

But this is never going to make a list of Top Ten Garden Tips. It is not neat or catchy, nor does it save obvious time or effort. It also smacks of a slightly smug self-righteousness and no one likes a smartarse. But, alas, it does tend to be true every time.

Planting out seedlings in plugs »

Growing

Grow for health – healthy soil, healthy plant, healthy animals, healthy garden, healthy ecosystem – healthy gardener. This does not mean that there will be no sickness, disasters or problems. Inevitably there will. But it does mean that there will be fewer and that recovery will be better and quicker.

Pay attention to every stage, every process. There is a tendency to focus on an end-result – harvest, flowering or an exhibition of some kind – but every part matters and every action contributes to every other action. Most failures in growth can be traced to carelessness at an early stage.

And try not to interrupt growth. Steady, unbroken growth will always result in stronger, healthier plants than spurts of intense activity. Sometimes the weather makes this very hard to achieve but that is even more reason not to contribute to erratic growth rates by forcing or delaying growth.

Timeliness is everything. The first stage is to study and learn this for every type of plant you grow so that you eventually learn when things should be done. Then you can progress to the next, and much more important, stage, which is to observe and respond so you intuitively know when to act even if, in some circumstances, it breaks every precedent or rule.

Fill bare soil. Bare soil looks empty, dries up fast, blows away in strong winds and then fills with weeds. Fill it with something. At the very least with mulch. However, annuals, groundcover, catchcrops, green manure will all do the job. Fill the ground.

Grow species. Man has bred plants over the centuries, always trying to 'improve' them for maximum impact. Occasionally this has produced plants that have enriched gardeners' lives and are unarguably better than either parent. But new plants are endlessly promoted by the horticultural trade in an effort to generate increased sales, and just because they are new, does not mean that they are any good – and almost invariably they are less beneficial to wildlife. Species plants are better for bees and most other insects because they have smaller flowers. They are usually less showy and flower for a shorter period than their hybridised offspring, but they often have a distinct elegance and charm, and are always robust and easier to grow.

Grow hard

Grow everything as tough as it will take from the very beginning of its life. The harder a plant is raised, the better it will adapt later on to the vagaries of weather, soil and season. But one plant's 'hard' is another's murder so use protection judiciously – but always the minimum necessary. Keep all greenhouses, tunnels and cold frames well ventilated and as cool as is consistent with steady growth or healthy winter dormancy.

Plants are tough. Leave them alone. Over-feeding, over-watering, over-protecting all do more harm than giving them a good home and leaving them to do what they do best – grow.

Everything you see above ground – your entire garden – is determined by what happens below ground level

Break the cycle of boom and bust. Forcing any plant into vigorous unnatural growth by dosing it with feed like a sickly Victorian child will always cause more harm than good. The results cannot be sustained. Any plant forced to grow beyond its means will sooner or later go bust. This might manifest itself in an attack by aphids or fungi, by poor uptake of water or nutrition, by its inability to support itself, or in a dozen other ways.

Grow good roots and the rest will follow. Everything you see above ground – your entire garden – is determined by what happens below ground level. All your efforts and skills should go into creating a really good root system and that will inevitably produce good foliage, flowers and fruit.

I was told many years ago not to worry too much about what did not get done in March or April because you could nearly always catch up in 'the back end', which refers to September and October. These have always been good gardening months and one of the (few) good things about climate change is that they are getting better. The light is fading but the heat remains in the soil and many, many plants flower, fruit and grow with a kind of serenity you do not find in any other season.

Be proud of your gardener's hands. Get your hands dirty. Handle the soil. Use your fingers to plant. Some people wear gloves to garden, but, short of a skin condition, something is lost.

Grow your own

Almost everything can be propagated vegetatively. Take cuttings, sow seed, sow indoors and out, sow direct, sow in seedbeds, split, divide, layer and graft.

Transplant self-sown seedlings wherever possible rather than raising or buying new ones. They will have already established a sophisticated relationship with the soil and will therefore grow extra healthily and fast.

Right plant, right place

Try and make every single plant in your garden feel at home. When you know where a plant originates from, you can see how it has evolved to adapt to that particular environment, be it a Chinese mountain valley, a Mediterranean hillside or a Welsh wood. Most plants are extraordinarily adaptable but approximating to their 'natural' habitat will always help.

It is uncanny how choosy and almost perverse some plants can be about their exact placement and how seemingly tiny variations will

Some plants will always find an unlikely home »

affect them. Do not hesitate to move a plant if it is not thriving. Find it a better home – which may be only a few feet away.

Plants find their own homes despite you. They will spread and self-seed in all kinds of contrary places. Leave them be. If they are happy, then so should you be.

What you grow matters much less than how you grow it. Plants are the ingredients, not the meal. There are very dull gardens full of fascinating plants and sublime gardens composed of a small selection of the most common plants available.

Trust yourself

Western horticulture has tended to elevate the specialist above the generalist. This is often unhelpful and inappropriate. Plantsmen and women are geeks. Like all geeks, they cannot imagine anyone not being as interested as they are by their own obsession. They are often charming and one can always learn from them but they are not typical gardeners, so do not be overly influenced or confused by them.

« The courtyard has a self-seeding square to offset its formality

Pruning

It is better not to prune at all than prune for the sake of it. No plant ever suffered through lack of pruning.

Work out exactly what you want as a result of pruning and try to understand how something grows before pruning. Does it flower on new or old wood? Does it grow new shoots in a great post-flowering burst or do they steadily emerge over the season? Does a fruit tree need to achieve a certain maturity to create spurs that bear fruit or will they be produced in the first year of growth? Does the plant heal well or is it, like cherries and plums, a bleeder – and if so when does it produce least sap? If in doubt about any of this, don't cut. Wait.

There is usually a right moment to prune any plant, when it will respond most beneficially for your purposes by producing more flowers, fruit, foliage or for training to shape, etc. But sometimes it is best to just do it. The worst that can happen is that you lose a season's flowering and even then you will have learned a useful lesson.

Timing of pruning

The pruning of flowering shrubs and trees should be based around the time of year that the flowers are produced. As a rule, plants that flower in the first half of the year – like *Clematis armandii, C. montana, C. alpina,* wisteria, ribes, forsythia and winter honeysuckle – do so on wood that has grown in the previous growing season, i.e. between spring and autumn. The safest time to prune them is immediately after flowering; if you prune them in winter or early spring, you will have plenty of new growth – but no flowers. This rule of thumb applies to all early-flowering trees, shrubs and climbers.

The exact opposite holds true for plants that flower in the second half of the year. They form their flower buds on new growth so you can afford to be ruthless in early spring and cut them back hard in the knowledge that this will instigate vigorous new growth, which in turn will carry all the flowering buds.

If you are not sure, don't prune this year; watch the plant, make notes and prune accordingly next year. The delay will not harm either you or the plant.

Shrubs like hydrangeas and lavender, especially in cold areas, are best left unpruned until you see new growth in spring, then cut back old stems but remove no more than a quarter of the living wood. They will look untidy over winter but the old growth gives them some protection from the cold.

How plants respond to pruning

It is worth understanding how plants respond to pruning. In all deciduous woody plants, food is stored in the roots over winter. As the leaves grow in spring, this stored food is taken to the leaves and stems where it is used, with any excess going back to the roots. The result of pruning means that when growth starts again, there is less demand on the food stored in the roots and more food to go round the remaining, unpruned parts of the plant. Consequently, these will grow with increased vigour, increased leaf size and longer internodal lengths (the space between leaves on the growing shoots).

> If you are not sure, don't prune this year; watch the plant, make notes and prune accordingly next year

The harder that you cut the main shoot, the more the side shoots will be stimulated to grow in response. The clearest effect of this is seen when you trim a hedge. Left unpruned it will be lank and straggly, but clipped regularly it will become increasingly twiggy and dense.

If you prune an apple tree hard each winter, it will make a mass of new growth but no flowers – and therefore no fruit. This cycle is often perpetuated by even harder pruning the following year – to get rid of all that new, fruitless growth, which, having lots of lovely succulent sap, will attract aphids and fungal disease. So, through over-zealous and mistimed pruning, people often ruin their fruit trees.

So the worst thing to do to any tree or shrub that is growing too vigorously for its situation, is to prune it hard in winter. If you wish to curtail its growth, leave the pruning to summer – July is ideal – when the foliage is fully grown and before the roots start to store food for winter.

Traditional advice was to paint any large wounds made by pruning, but current thinking is that this does more harm than good as it seals in moisture and disease. By far the best course is to leave a clean cut and let it heal over itself.

Winter pruning

Although winter pruning can start at any time from November and continue until the middle of March, I have a basic rule for my timing of it: I do not begin it until the leaves have fallen and I do not continue once the leaves start to reappear.

Fruit trees: Prune any crossing or rubbing branches. Cut back any overlong or straggly branches to a bud to promote vigorous multi-stemmed regrowth. Do not prune plums, apricots, peaches or cherries in winter; these should be pruned in late spring and only if absolutely necessary.

Trained fruit (cordons, espaliers, fans): You must act counter-intuitively with these. Remember that the harder you cut, the stronger the regrowth, so cut back any weak growth to encourage vigorous new shoots in spring.

Soft fruit: Cut back autumn-fruiting raspberries to the ground, removing all of last year's canes. Cut away all crossing and inward-

Pruning the pleached limes in early spring »

growing stems from redcurrants and gooseberries to create an open goblet shape. Reduce remaining growth by a third to create a strong framework of branches.

Roses: Pruning the roses should always be a key part of your winter pruning programme. In my garden it is a job that I usually do in February (see page 211) but the conditions in yours may allow you to prune your roses a little earlier or a little later. My rule is, though, that I do not prune once the leaves have started back into growth.

Shrubs: Buddleia, cornus, willows, spiraea, deciduous ceanothus, *Fuchsia fulgens* and *F. magellanica* can all be cut hard back just like late-flowering clematis (see page 213). The harder they are cut, the more they will flower.

Clematis should be mulched generously after pruning and in fact, any flowering climber or shrub is best watered and mulched when you have finished pruning.

....

Summer pruning

Evergreens, shrubs that flower on old wood, trained fruit and established hedges should all be pruned in the summer.

Espalier fruit are the perfect example. In winter I prune my espalier pears to encourage new shoots and I know that the harder I cut them back, the stronger and therefore better the growth will be the following summer. But in summer (which in practice means any time in July and August) I reduce all new upright growth from the fruiting spurs down to a healthy couple of spurs (which will produce next year's fruits) and any other growth that goes outside the limitations of the parallel rows of the espalier. This applies to fan-trained, step-over and cordon fruit, as well as to any large apple or pear trees that have become too crowded and overgrown. The result is a streamlined, less shaggy version, with plenty of light and air reaching the ripening fruit.

Deadheading is a form of summer pruning and its main purpose is to stimulate side shoots and therefore more flowers.

Topiary

Topiary is really nothing more than fancy pruning. It is most effective when made from evergreen plants with small leaves that respond well to being clipped hard. There are a number that do this job well, such as box, privet and small-leafed honeysuckle, *Lonicera nitida*, but the best is undoubtedly yew. This will grow in any soil but does need good drainage, so if you have heavy clay, add plenty of grit to the soil before planting.

> # It is much easier to train young plants and grow them into a shape than to try and 'carve' topiary from an existing plant

Topiary can be solemn and formal but is a traditional feature of a cottage garden – where it has its tongue firmly in its cheek. There is an element of sandcastle-building, pomposity held in check by the knowledge that time and tide will wash this work and all potential pretensions away.

It is much easier to train young plants and grow them into a shape than to try and 'carve' topiary from an existing plant. This is because you have to clip topiary regularly for it to become firm and self-supporting. Remember that the harder a stem is cut back, the more vigorous its responding growth will be. If, on the other hand, you wish a single shoot to become a feature such as a limb or a head, then leave it unpruned until it has reached the desired length.

You can train a plant into a complicated shape by using canes to hold young stems in position until they have become sufficiently hard to support themselves. You can also place a 'former' over the young plant, made from chicken wire or other self-supporting wire or metal construct, and as the new growth appears beyond it, cut it back to the outlines of the former, finally removing it before it becomes inextricably entwined.

Hedges

1. **Cutting** hedges is just another form of pruning.
2. **Summer** hedge trimmings can be mown and added straight to the compost heap. Winter hedge trimmings can be shredded and used as material for temporary paths.
3. **Summer-cut** hedges will stay shorter longer. Winter-cut hedges will grow back thicker and faster.
4. **Never** cut hedges hard between February and late July to avoid disturbing nesting birds. Keep it to the lightest trim but always go into winter – November – with freshly cut hedges. It sets the garden straight.

« The annual summer hedge trim tightens the whole garden; this is repeated with a second cut in October to keep it sharp all winter

Food

Grow your own. I have yet to meet a single person who does not agree that any food, carefully grown, picked when ready and in its due season, and eaten absolutely fresh does not taste better than food, however glossily packaged, from a shop. The satisfaction of sowing seed, raising the little seedlings, thinning, watering, weeding and ultimately harvesting the final product when it is exactly at its best, and then serving it to be eaten with family and friends, is matched by few other pleasures in life.

Those first new potatoes or baby broad beans, carrots pulled direct from the ground or a lettuce cut, washed and eaten within the hour, are foods fit for kings – and yet are all within the grasp of anybody with a scrap of land to sow some seeds into.

The satisfaction of growing your own, harvesting the product when it is exactly at its best and then eating it with family and friends, is matched by few other pleasures in life

What is more, you ingest more than just produce. You become nourished by the earth, by your labour, by the intimate and unbroken connection with the ingredients themselves, and by the profound satisfaction of knowing that no one in an office constructed that meal as part of a profit-forecast spreadsheet – let alone used and abused labourers, and abased them for a pitiful wage.

Whilst self-sufficiency is inevitably doomed to humiliating failure, self-provision elevates the grower to self-esteem and a world of small

Few meals taste as good as those made from home-grown ingredients »

166

but profoundly influential pleasures. A perfectly ripe pear, garlic eaten fresh from the earth, a sun-warmed tomato and peas shucked from a crisp pod are all big deals. It costs a lot to buy that satisfaction – more than you and I usually have access to. So by buying into it rather than paying out to an anonymous, cynical provider, we free ourselves of that particular tyranny.

Eat your garden

Make meals from what you gather rather than gather specific ingredients to complete a recipe. Check your edible garden daily with a basket over your arm as though wandering through a wonderful Mediterranean market, seeing what is best or what inspires you, checking it for ripeness and then working out how best to use what you have selected.

The long litany of vegetable seeds and all their varieties can be intimidating. Combine this with the rules of crop rotation, soil requirements and seasonal vagaries, and it becomes downright confusing. There is only one solution: grow what you would like to eat.

And grow to taste the difference, too. Maincrop potatoes are relatively easy and cheap to buy and often very good. But new potatoes are incomparably better when eaten within hours of harvesting, so your own home-grown ones will always be much better than any you can buy. This is also true of asparagus, sweetcorn, pears, strawberries, carrots, rocket, most salad crops and fresh peas. It might well be so with most vegetables, but maximise the freshness and seasonality of your garden rather than just going through the motions of raising a wide selection.

Consume what is fresh and in season and be grateful for its time rather than intolerant of its unseasonal absence.

Surplus and succession

Raise 10–25 per cent more seedlings than you might need. This will cover disaster and also provide replacements. But once the main body of seedlings has got established, give the excess away or consign them to the compost heap. Be prepared but be ruthless.

Grow all vegetables to perfect ripeness. Baby veg are an absurd indulgence. This is to do with maturity as well as size. Not too big but not too small. If you want slightly smaller vegetables, grow them a little closer together or choose a variety that is smaller. But to eat vegetables at the seedling stage is decadent and wasteful.

Grow heritage vegetables. Seeds are a measure of resilience through their diversity rather than abundance. We should have as varied and localised a range of varieties and species as we possibly can – and did have until the second half of the twentieth century. So find heritage varieties, collect, keep and share their seeds. They might be hard to get hold of initially – but try.

Succession is smart (see page 174). It is tempting to grow a bumper crop and sometimes unavoidable – tomatoes, maincrop potatoes, pumpkins, most fruit lend themselves to this – but try and manage succession as cleverly as you can. This means planting and sowing a small amount of seed a number of times throughout the growing season. The changing light levels and temperatures mean that this cannot be done at regular intervals so you must take into account varying speeds of growth and ripening as the seasons shift. Hence the need to pay attention and be a little smart about it.

Growing conditions

It is better to be too late than too early. Be patient. Wait until the soil and you are ready for each other. There is nearly always time to catch up. I have had really good years in my vegetable garden when I did not sow a seed before the beginning of May.

When growing vegetables, it is the combination of temperature and moisture that fosters or hinders growth. You can do nothing about the weather and you cannot change your basic soil type, but try to influence what is possible and do not struggle against that which you cannot change.

Plenty of vegetables, like all the brassicas, chicories, chards, Japanese

greens and root crops like swedes and turnips, will cope with quite cold temperatures and still continue to develop.

Like rhubarb, some vegetables such as Florence fennel, celery, celeriac, squashes and courgettes, need lots of water to grow well. But no vegetables like being cold and wet.

The answer is to improve drainage and water retention by adding lots of compost to your soil. If your plot is heavy clay, try mixing in as much grit as you can. Avoid standing on the soil, which creates compaction and worsens drainage. And invest in fleece – which can be used to warm up the soil before sowing – and some cloches to act as umbrellas to keep the soil dry as well as trapping any sun.

If it is very hot and dry, you need to water regularly so some kind of water-collection system is a good idea. We use cattle drinking troughs because we can dip watering cans into them, but you can get water butts in many shapes and sizes. A standpipe is also a good investment, and worth putting in before the garden gets too established.

Gardening is wellbeing

We use the expression 'being grounded' or 'keeping your feet on the ground' to indicate being in touch with reality, keeping ourselves honest. I feel exactly the same way about having my hands in the soil. It keeps me true and rooted.

When we grow something – anything at all – it can never be 'ours' in anything other than an adoptive way. It exists independent of us and we share it with anyone and everyone who sees or consumes it with us. I think that this sharing process is what completes the truly healing circle of a close, intimate connection with the soil. If our own personal batteries are charged by it, then it is equally important that there is a social charge, too, and one that we do not need to intellectualise to share and benefit from.

Grow good vegetables with honest hands, make a meal that is shared around a table, and you have the bedrock, the essence of wellbeing.

« Raised beds are ideal for vegetables, especially if your soil is heavy

Grow Your Own Veg

When I was a boy, it was very normal for gardeners to be almost self-sufficient in vegetables. This was a hangover from the war and the Dig-For-Victory mentality, where you either grew your own or went without. But in my lifetime, supermarkets, offering every fruit and vegetable every day of the year, have been all that a whole generation has come to know. Clingfilm-wrapped, unripe, seasonless food is convenient and provides instant gratification but it is far from the deeply satisfying reality of home-grown produce.

But things are starting to change. More and more people are wanting allotments and more people are beginning to recognise the virtues and joys of growing some vegetables in their own garden if they have one. People are even growing herbs in pots on windowsills, vegetables in window boxes and fruit on trellises in the smallest garden, and as well as enjoying the gardening, are getting to realise how good their own produce can taste!

Anyone who starts to grow vegetables discovers that it is an enormously pleasurable, rewarding pastime. It is fun. I have seen spritely 90-year-olds digging on allotments and three-year-olds helping plant a row of beans. Not only does growing your own keep you physically well and fit, but all evidence shows that it plays a remarkably effective role in both countering and healing mental illness. Getting out there, with dirt on your hands and the sun on your back, and connecting with the rhythms of the natural world, is the best possible medicine.

No garden is too small. A window box or pot is ideal for herbs that will transform many dishes and a square yard of ground will produce a regular supply of salad leaves throughout the year.

What is more, vegetables can be as decorative as any flower border and a healthy vegetable patch filled with produce is always beautiful. The French potager makes a virtue of this, with beds bounded by clipped box hedges, with roses and herbs and climbing beans, and with sweet peas and gourds trailing over wigwams or trellises. Do not hide the kitchen garden away but enjoy its display in all seasons and make it a proud feature of your garden. The main thing to remember is that vegetables grow best in good soil that is rich with organic matter and is free-draining with direct sun for at least half the day and preferably longer.

The secret is to keep it simple. It is not a test or competition and should never feel like a tyranny. Sprinkle some seeds onto the warming spring soil, thin them as the seedlings grow, keep them watered and weeded, and harvest them in their season.

....

Getting started

One of the skills of growing good vegetables at home lies in paying attention to and working with the particular conditions on your plot. You cannot cheat the weather. If the soil is cold to the touch, then few seeds will germinate. A good rule of thumb is that if the weeds are not growing, then it is too cold for your vegetable seeds.

As soon as your soil is dry enough to rake without the soil sticking to the tines, and does not feel cold to touch, you can start by sowing parsnips, broad beans, rocket and spinach, and can place onion and shallot sets, burying them so that their tops are clear of the ground.

However you sow, always be careful to do so as thinly as possible and thin the seedlings as soon as they are large enough to handle, so that you are left with a row of maturing plants about 3–9in apart.

If we get a bout of cold spring weather, seedlings can emerge and then stop growing, and then they are very susceptible to snails and slugs. But even if it is wet and cold outside, you can sow seeds in spring under cover in a seed tray or in plugs, in peat-free compost. A greenhouse is best, but cold frames are very good, and a porch or windowsill are perfectly workable, too. When your seedlings are a reasonable size, put them outside to harden off for a week or two before planting them out when the soil is warm at 6–9in spacing and when they are big enough to withstand any kind of slug or snail attack.

Succession sowing

Succession is the key for the most productive vegetable patch and gives a steady supply of fresh vegetables for as long as possible. What this means is sowing batches of your favourite vegetables in two or three goes across the growing season, so that as one batch is coming to the end, another is just ready to be harvested, with perhaps a third batch being sown or grown on.

Obviously, this takes a little organisation. Start with a small amount of fast-growing salad leaves raised indoors in plugs so they can be planted out as soon as the ground warms up, and follow these with regular sowings, both raised in plugs and directly sown, right through to September.

Crops like peas and beans, chard, carrots and beetroot grow more slowly but can be spread over several months to provide two or three overlapping waves of harvest.

Finally, there are the long, slow crops like most brassicas, chicory, garlic or celery that are going to tie up space for most of the growing year. I always interplant these with a catch-crop like radish or rocket that can be eaten before they start to compete with the slow-growers.

Soil and crop rotation

The best soil is high in humus or organic matter from the roots of plants and the addition of decaying plant material such as compost or manure. Once the soil is in very good condition, all it needs is a top-up of a mulch or an inch or two of compost once, or at most twice a year, but it may take a few years to reach that state of soil heaven.

So assess your soil and if it is very sandy, it will need lots of organic material to give it a better structure and hold more nutrients and moisture. Likewise, if it is clay and very heavy, adding organic matter will open it out and improve drainage. If you cannot dig, then a mulch laid on the surface will do the job and work itself into the soil, albeit a little more slowly.

Red and green oak-leaf lettuce look as good as they taste! »

Root crops such as carrots and parsnips grow best in soil that is very free-draining and that has not had fresh organic material added to it in the past year. This is because it can cause the roots to bifurcate and split, as well as encouraging lush foliage growth at the expense of the roots.

So it is common practice to heavily enrich one third of the plot, which is ideal for potatoes and all legumes as well as salad crops, and to top up another third with a mulch of good compost, which is good for all brassicas like cabbages, cauliflowers and broccoli, and also alliums like onions, leeks and garlic. The third section is left unenriched and used for root crops.

Root crops such as carrots and parsnips grow best in soil that is very free-draining

It is easiest to manage this as a regular rotation. So in the first year of the rotation, the first third is manured heavily, the second third lightly, and the last one left untouched. In the next year, this last third becomes the first, so is heavily enriched; last year's first third now gets a top up and the third that was second last year, and had brassicas and alliums as the main crop, is left alone to grow carrots and roots. And so it goes.

In practice there is much more mixing and matching than that, and crops are squeezed in amongst each other. The rule is not made to be slavishly obeyed and can be bent and even broken, but it is a good guiding principle.

Raised beds

Raised beds are perfect if you have limited space or mobility. They are also the best way of coping with very poor or thin soil. For many years I had raised beds that were simply mounds of soil. They worked well but the soil did spill onto the paths, which is why having a solid edging is better. I have found recycled scaffolding planks are cheap and ideal.

Do not be tempted to make raised beds too wide: 5ft is the maximum workable width. It is also best to keep them to less than 15ft long so that they are quick and easy to walk around.

Mark the beds out with string and dig the ground deeply, adding as much manure or compost as you can obtain. This will raise the surface of the soil. You can also fork over the paths and shovel a layer of topsoil from them onto the beds, or topsoil can be bought in if necessary. The greater depth of topsoil means a better root run and improved drainage, and the soil will be noticeably quicker to warm up in spring.

Use bark chippings, paving or grass for the paths. Rake over and top-dress the beds with a layer of compost, and they are ready for planting or sowing.

You should be able to reach everything from the paths without ever having to stand on the bed itself, so every square inch of the beds can be planted. This also means that once made, the beds need no further cultivation at all. Heavy rain can cause compaction but the addition of compost will encourage earthworm activity, which is enough to keep the soil open. I always have a length of scaffolding board cut so it rests firmly on the outside edging boards of the raised beds, so I can stand or kneel on that when planting rather than on the soil. But most of the time you should be able to reach anything you want from the paths.

Essential veg

Grow what you love to eat. The kitchen should dictate what is in the garden rather than the garden deciding what is on your plate. However, I have found the following six vegetables to be essential:

Tomatoes: A ripe tomato eaten warm from the sun is the real thing. Tomatoes do need as much sun as possible and are always better in a greenhouse, porch or conservatory if possible.

Lettuce/rocket: I love fresh salad leaves and it is easy to grow them in succession so you can cut fresh leaves every day of the year. If I had to choose two, it would be peppery, succulent rocket in the cool months and then a crisp Cos lettuce in summer.

Chard: Versatile, robust and delicious, Swiss chard is as good in midwinter as it is in midsummer. The leaves can be cooked like spinach and the stems are superb in stir-fries or with a sauce. It will regrow after cutting.

Garlic: Garlic falls between vegetables and herbs but lately I grow a lot of Elephant garlic – which is strictly a type of leek – and would now not be without it. Not only is it delicious and easy to store for months, but it is also extremely good for you.

Kale: If I only grew one brassica it would be this. Black Tuscan kale – cavolo nero – is a permanent fixture in my veg patch. The plants can be harvested for 10 months of the year, taste zingy and fresh, and improve after a frost.

New potatoes: Maincrop potatoes are prone to blight and are very easy to buy, but new potatoes quickly lose their sweetness, so your own, eaten fresh from the soil, are sweeter and nicer than any from a shop.

Slugs and snails

Slugs and snails perform an invaluable role in recycling waste vegetative matter and are an essential part of a compost heap. The problem is that they do not discriminate between a fallen leaf and a delicious young seedling. They love young, soft tissue. So the trick is to make it available for as short a time as possible.

Resist sowing or planting tender plants too soon. Any plant that is stressed by bad weather, erratic watering or, in particular, overfeeding, will be the first to be attacked. Harden off plants well (see page 224) and do not overfeed. This will avoid a spurt of the soft, sappy growth that slugs love. You want your plants to be tough and able to withstand hardship but not ill and run-down. Remember that the healthiest plants are those that respond best to the situation that they grow in –

whatever and wherever it might be.

Encourage a wide range of predators to get rid of pests for you. Thrushes, frogs, toads, beetles, centipedes, shrews and hedgehogs all love eating slugs and snails. Encouraging predators means giving them plenty of cover, an avoidance of toxic chemicals – such as slug pellets – and a degree of tolerance for collateral damage.

Vegetable growing at a glance

1. **Choose** a sunny site protected from cold winds.
2. **Prepare** the soil well and look after it lovingly; raised beds are very effective and an efficient use of space.
3. **Make** a compost heap and regard good compost as your best ally.
4. **Grow** crops in succession, aiming at a steady supply for as long as possible rather than periods of glut and famine.
5. **Keep** on top of weeds by weeding little and often. Mulch bare soil to suppress weed growth.
6. **Learn** to be ruthless and thin seedlings at an early stage so you develop strong healthy plants rather than lots of small ones.
7. **The** best protection from pests and disease is to grow healthy plants, and the healthiest plants are those that have adapted best to the conditions. Grow hard, do not mollycoddle or overfeed, but do not expose young plants to unnecessary stress.
8. **Grow** what you love to eat.

Grow Your Own Herbs

In many ways, herbs are the easiest and best plants to grow in your garden. This is partly because many herbs lend themselves to growing in poor soil and in containers, but also because just a few plants can transform and improve a whole range of other cooking ingredients. Fresh herbs truly can be part of any home.

They are very forgiving plants to grow. Many of our favourites, like rosemary, thyme and sage, come from the baking hills of the Mediterranean and do best in poor soil. Others, like parsley, coriander, basil and dill, are annuals that grow fast and easily.

Mediterranean herbs

This group includes culinary herbs such as rosemary, thyme, sage, tarragon, coriander, bay and oregano. Decorative and medicinal herbs such as lavender, santolina, artemisia and hyssop share the same growing conditions.

You must be cruel to be kind to these plants. Always add drainage to your soil and never add compost or manure. If you grow them in pots, mix ordinary peat-free potting compost with the same volume of sharp sand or grit.

Do not feed them as the harder they are grown, the better able they are to resist problems of weather, pests or disease. However, do not forget to water them in summer, and although they can dry out in winter, as long as they are not too wet, they are very hardy. But the combination of wet and cold is often fatal.

Annual herbs

Like any other annual plants, annual herbs do all their growing, flowering and – critically – seed production – within one growing season. Many then promptly die, although some can live on for a few more years. But the gardener can harness this speed of production through managing seeds. Sow them in spring and you will have a crop. Sow some every few months and you have more than a crop – you have a daily supply.

Sow some every few months and you have more than a crop – you have a daily supply

My favourite annual herbs are basil, parsley and coriander. Basil is tender so needs protection from frost. It is, however, a very robust, strong-growing plant that needs plenty of space to develop properly and that can be picked over all summer long to provide fresh leaves.

I grow mine alongside tomatoes in the greenhouse from May onwards, and outside in the garden once the nights get reliably warm in July, allowing at least 6in between each seedling.

Parsley and coriander are robust plants that will grow in some shade. I grow both all the year round, inside and out, making a sowing every few months.

Summer herbs from seed

Growing your own herbs from seed is easy, very cheap and will provide a household with a really abundant supply of delicious herbs.

They don't all share the same exact cultivation requirements but you will not go far wrong with a sprinkle of seed in a seed tray or pot, using a peat-free seed compost. A step more sophisticated is to sow into plugs, which makes transplanting much easier and more successful. Early in the year this should be done in a greenhouse, cold frame or on a windowsill.

Once the seedlings emerge, it is important to thin them so that each one has the space to grow into a healthy plant. When you buy a ready-grown pot of herbs such as basil or parsley, there will be dozens of

seedlings crammed into one pot, which gives the appearance of abundance. But to grow strong plants that will last a long time, you must give each seedling room to develop in a plug or pot of its own. Either transplant them out into the garden or grow them on in pots, keeping them watered but not soggy.

....

Perennial herbs

Some herbs are herbaceous perennials that survive the winter by their top growth all dying back in autumn and by growing fresh foliage and flowers in spring and summer. My own favourites from this group are mint, chives, lovage, marjoram, fennel, sorrel, tarragon and horseradish.

Mint: There are many different mints but the three to grow for the kitchen are spearmint (*Mentha spicata*), peppermint (*M.* x *piperita*) and apple mint (*M. suaveolens*). Mint grows in most soils and conditions although it prefers a rather damp, sunny site. However, it will spread invasively if given the chance, so I recommend growing it in a container.

Chives: These are an allium, like garlic, and are very easy to grow from seed. They become long-lived perennials that can be chopped into sections with a spade to create new plants, each capable of regrowing with fresh vigour. The flowers are beautiful and also edible, but cut them back right to the ground as soon as the blooms start to fade, and they will very quickly grow new shoots. This can be repeated every four weeks or so throughout the growing season.

Lovage: This has very deep, fleshy roots and does best in fairly moist soil. The leaves have a subtle and delicious celery flavour that is very good in soups and stews. It grows very large with a giant flower head that should be cut back with some of the older leaves at least once in summer to encourage fresh growth.

« Thyme thriving in well-drained soil

Marjoram: *Origanum vulgare* is called marjoram in the UK and oregano in the Mediterranean. It is very hardy and will grow in part-shade although is happiest with full sun and free drainage and dislikes acid soil. Bees love the pale mauve flowers.

Sweet marjoram (*O. majorana*) is less hardy but more aromatic. We grow French marjoram (*O.* x *onites*), which has green leaves, and golden marjoram (*O. vulgare* 'Aureum'). The French marjoram is very robust and adaptable but, like thyme, the secret is to have it unshaded and to keep cutting it back hard to encourage fresh new leaves.

Fennel: Fennel (*Foeniculum vulgare*) will seed itself freely and bronze fennel (*F. v.* 'Purpureum') is a welcome self-seeder all over my garden. The seedlings have a deep taproot so must be transplanted when very young if they are to survive the move. The leaves and seeds of fennel are delicious with any fish or pork.

Sorrel: This is another shade- and damp-loving herb, with a distinct lemony astringency, especially good in early spring and with egg dishes of any kind. Common sorrel (*Rumex acetosa*) is spinach-like and best eaten cooked, but French sorrel (*R. scutatus*) has smaller, less bitter leaves and is better used in salads.

Tarragon: The slim, pointed, glaucous leaves of tarragon are deceptive because there are two kinds that look similar but have very different virtues for the gardener and cook. French tarragon (*Artemisia dracunculus*) has superb flavour and is the ideal accompaniment to any chicken or fish dish. It makes a woody shrub that likes good drainage and sunshine but it is not hardy and hates cold, wet weather. I dig mine up in autumn, cut it back hard and store it in a pot within the protection of a greenhouse, planting it back out again after the last frost.

Russian tarragon (*A. dracunculoides*) is much hardier and more adaptable, and will grow outside in most winters but its taste is so inferior to its French counterpart that it is not worth growing for culinary use.

Horseradish: Horseradish (*Armoracia rusticana*) has large, luxuriant leaves in summer but it is an herbaceous perennial so the leaves will have completely disappeared by mid-December. However, the long taproots are still there beneath the soil and it is these roots that are grated and used to make the familiar fiery sauce.

If you dig the roots up in late summer, they still taste relatively mild but by Christmas, when the leaves have died right back, the roots should be treated with the same care as chilli. They should be scrubbed, peeled and then grated into a bowl before mixing with cream, salt and pepper and perhaps a dash of lemon juice or white wine vinegar. This sauce can be heated (which will make it milder) and served with an oily fish or can be served cold with beef.

Horseradish can become a weed if not restricted to an odd corner but it is easier to dig up in lighter soil. New plants grow very easily from root cuttings. Dig up some good, straight roots, cut them into 2–3in lengths, pot them up until new growth appears, and then plant outside.

Grow Your Own
Top Fruit

'Top fruit' refers to any fruit that is produced on trees, although the 'trees' are often easily pruned and trained to fit into very small spaces indeed by training as step-overs, espaliers, cordons or fans, or by growing on dwarf rootstocks.

I know that a lot of people are scared of growing fruit. They think that it takes great expertise in pruning and pollinating, and are confused by rootstocks, fruit groups, disease and pests. But growing fruit is not just good fun, it is also easy.

A key tip for all fruit trees is to keep them clear of grass and weeds for a diameter of at least 3ft around the trunk – and ideally twice that. Mulch thickly each year. This will do more than anything else to keep them healthy.

Apples

All apples need a pollinator growing within about 100 yards, so either grow two trees or check that there are apples growing in your neighbours' gardens. Apples flower from about the middle of April to the middle of May, with each tree's blossom lasting about 10 days. This means that they do not all overlap and cannot all pollinate each other, so make sure that your trees flower at the same time.

Shelter from cold winds is vital, as is sun for ripening as well as good drainage.

Summer pruning in July and August will restrict growth and is used for training trees. Winter pruning, between November and March, will encourage vigorous regrowth around and below each cut.

Apples are grown on rootstocks, which determine the size of the tree. M9 is best for containers and very small trees, MM106 best for medium-sized trees, cordons and espaliers, and poorish soil, and MM111 is ideal for larger trees.

Varieties: There are over 600 wonderful varieties of apple so I urge plenty of apple-eating homework! However, my personal favourites are, for eating, 'Jupiter', 'Ribston Pippin' and 'Rosemary Russet'; and for cooking, 'Blenheim Orange', 'Arthur Turner', 'Newton Wonder'.

Pears

Pears will tolerate slightly colder, damper growing conditions than apples, although the fruit needs more sun to ripen. They are ideal to grow against a sunny wall or fence and are best trained as espaliers, which they very easily respond to. With all training of fruit trees, it is worth remembering that fruit in general is produced most abundantly on lateral growth, whereas the tree most wants to grow vertically. Reducing vertical growth and training horizontally encourages fruit but loses vigour.

Varieties: 'Doyenné du Comice', 'Williams' Bon Chrétien', 'Beth'.

Plums

Plums ripen from midsummer into autumn, and include damsons and greengages as variations on the plum theme. They grow well in a soil that is heavier and wetter than that needed by most fruits – with damsons being exceptionally hardy and greengages needing a sheltered, sunny site. But all plums ripen best in full sun, with only 'Czar' and 'Victoria' growing successfully in shade.

Because the blossom is among the first to appear, plums are very susceptible to frost damage and this is often the cause of a lack of fruit. Plum trees do not need any pruning but if necessary, it should be done in June and in dry weather.

Varieties: 'Victoria', 'Oullins Golden Gage', 'Czar'.

Quinces

Quinces look like a curious hybrid of apple and pear, and although rock-hard and inedible when raw, are fragrantly delicious cooked either as a fruit or a jelly. Quinces make a small tree with an ungainly tangle of branches that resists training and with the most lovely, fragrant blossom of all. They do not need pruning and are self-fertile, so a single tree will usually bear fruit after a few years. They like moist soil but do best in a warm spot.

Varieties: 'Vranja', 'Leskovac', 'Champion'.

Peaches and nectarines

Peaches and nectarines share the same growing conditions. The trees are very hardy but blossom early, so are susceptible to late frosts. They like rich soil with lots of water but will not tolerate waterlogging. They also need a heavy mulch of good compost every year. Both will grow well in a large container. And both are very prone to peach leaf curl, caused by fungus, but are remarkably resilient and will produce healthy new leaves later in the season.

For the fruit to ripen, they need a sunny wall or fence and some protection against frost that can be removed in good weather – a canopy of fleece works well. Fruits are formed on new growth, so they can be pruned hard every year, removing at least a third of all shoots. They also respond well to fan-training. It is important to thin the fruits so none touches or shades another.

Varieties: 'Duke of York', 'Peregrine', 'Lord Napier' (nectarine).

Apricots

Apricots grow very like peaches but the blossom is even earlier, so must have some protection. Although fully ripe apricots are delicious,

« A harvest of 'Vranja' quinces from one tree

in this country apricots are best used for jam. But what wonderful jam! The trees are tough and pest-free if they are grown well with rich, free-draining soil and a thick mulch each spring. Prune out all dead and damaged branches and summer-prune to restrict growth.

Varieties: 'Moorpark' (best), 'Hemskerke' (for cold areas).

Figs

Figs need as much sunshine as possible to ripen fully, which makes them ideal for training against a sunny wall. They need well-drained soil with plenty of moisture and, once established, their roots should be restricted by a wall or some underground barrier. This will encourage more fruit and less tree.

> # A key tip for all fruit trees is to keep them clear of grass and weeds for a diameter of at least 3ft around the trunk, and mulch thickly each year

The fruits are produced on the previous year's growth so pruning, which is best done in spring, should be to shape and train, and encourage the next year's crop. Figs carry at least two and sometimes three crops of fruit at once with two harvests in warm conditions, but in Britain, only one will ripen a year. So once the last mature fruit has been gathered at the end of October, all figs bigger than a pea should be removed and composted.

Figs will grow perfectly well in a container, although they will need repotting every couple of years or so and feeding with liquid seaweed every week in the growing season.

Figs are self-fertile so you only need to plant one to get fruit. 'Brown Turkey' is the variety that you are most likely to find in a garden centre and it is certainly the fig that is most likely to ripen outdoors in all but the warmest and most protected British gardens.

Varieties: 'Brown Turkey', 'Ischia', 'Brunswick'.

....

Morello cherries

The morello cherry is sour so it is used for cooking and preserving rather than eating raw. Although grown widely in this country by Tudor times, – to the extent that by 1640 over two dozen named cultivars were recorded – morello cherries were not widely eaten until supplies of cheap sugar started to arrive in this country in the middle of the eighteenth century from the new West Indian colonies. This meant that the sour fruit could be sweetened and properly appreciated.

Unlike most sweet cherries, morello cherries are self-fertile so will crop reliably. They grow well in shade and are ideal for training as a fan against an east- or north-facing wall. They bear their fruit on the previous year's growth so should be pruned in early summer whilst this year's crop is still unripe, removing excess side shoots and leaving those that remain ready to carry next year's fruit.

....

Fruit training styles

Espalier is where all but parallel layers of lateral branches are cut off. Fruiting spurs grow up from the lateral branches and everything apart from necessary new growth is pruned back each summer. Espaliers can be grown against a wall or fence, or in the open so you can easily pick from both sides. It is an extremely effective way of growing fruit and looks wonderful, but needs strong support, unless well-established.
Cordon is where each tree is reduced to a single stem with fruiting spurs along its length. They are normally grown at 45 degrees for a balance of horizontal and vertical growth. It is an excellent way of growing a lot of varieties in a limited space. Cordons need permanent support.
Fan has a central stem from which splay out diagonal stems, each bearing fruit. This must have a strong fence or wall with fixed wires to tie the fan-trained fruit to. It is commonly used for figs, peaches, nectarines and cherries.

Grow Your Own Soft Fruit

I love eating and growing as much fruit as possible in its proper season. Gooseberry fool in June, summer pudding in July made from freshly picked blackcurrants and redcurrants (and perhaps raspberries but never, ever strawberries. Very wrong). Strawberries eaten warm from the hot July soil. A ripe pear in September and an October apple plucked from the tree, ripe and crispy and with a deep complexity of flavour.

Soft fruit produces some of the easiest and least troublesome edible crops that can be grown, although I suspect that many gardeners feel that they do not have space for them. But this is not the case. Cottagers always grew currants and gooseberries because they are tough, delicious, almost entirely maintenance-free and can be eaten and stored in lots of different ways whilst always remaining a treat. All those qualities remain today and you only need a bush or two to have a surprising quantity of fruit. Soft fruit is also wonderfully decorative – think of jewel-like beads of redcurrants or the rich stems of rhubarb.

The biggest problem is blackbirds and thrushes stealing the fruit as it ripens, but a temporary netting will solve that, and if you are very keen, a permanent fruit cage provides a safe haven for every type of fruit.

Rhubarb

Rhubarb likes a deep, rich, but not boggy soil. It can take any amount of frost but the crowns need mulching to stop them drying out (although keep the mulch clear of the crowns themselves so that they

Once you have tasted warm, homegrown strawberries,
nothing else is ever as good »

do not rot if it is very wet). Rhubarb can not only tolerate cold weather but needs some to trigger it into stem production.

The earliest rhubarb can be forced by depriving the emerging shoots of light with an upturned bucket or an old chimney pot sealed with a tile, but spring is its natural season. The early, forced pickings may be sweetest but a basket of thick, mature crimson rhubarb looks good enough to display in a vase.

Currants

Redcurrants: Redcurrants are perhaps the easiest fruit of all to grow. They will grow in nearly every soil and position, coping with almost total shade or an exposed, open site. They can be trained as cordons or fans, or grown as a bush, and for a small garden, they make an ideal cover for a north wall or fence.

The fruit hangs like bunches of ruby beads on spurs on two- or three-year-old wood so, having decided on how they are to be grown, annual pruning is geared to creating and maintaining a permanent framework of branches.

Redcurrants will grow in nearly every soil and position, coping with almost total shade or an exposed, open site

Their biggest pest is the sawfly, which lays its eggs at the base of the plant. These then hatch and the larvae gradually work their way to the end of the branches, eating every leaf they come across. The answer is to grow the bushes as an open goblet – ideally on a central stem or 'leg' so that the whole bush is raised a foot off the ground.

In late winter, prune any inward-growing branches and reduce new growth by a third so that you are left with the woody bowl-like frame.

« Redcurrants

This exposes the centre of the bush and deters the fly from laying its eggs, as well as making any of the larvae easy to spot and pick off.

White currants are essentially albino versions of redcurrants and are grown in exactly the same way.

Blackcurrants: Blackcurrants are very different to red- and white currants. For a start, they respond in direct relationship to the richness of the soil, so add lots of manure or compost to the ground before planting and mulch thickly with more of the same every year. They also need sunshine for the new wood and fruit to ripen.

In short, gooseberries (see below), red- and white currants can be fitted in around the demands of other plants and designs, but blackcurrants must take a choice spot to flourish.

Blackcurrants also produce their fruit on new wood rather than on two-year-old spurs. In the first year they produce some fruit, lots in the second year and the crop begins to fall off thereafter. So the pruning regime is to remove a third of each bush, down to the ground, every year immediately after the last fruit is collected.

Birds love all these currants, especially redcurrants, so they must be netted from the time that the berries start to ripen to the last picking – about mid-June till mid-August – or else the entire crop can be stripped overnight.

Berries

Gooseberries: The secret of good gooseberries is to treat 'em rough. Resist feeding or mollycoddling them but take care to prune them so that plenty of air and light can get to every branch – this will also make picking less of a prickly business.

They are even more prone to sawfly than the redcurrants, so prune them in the same way – as open goblets – and give them an open, exposed position. This also helps against American mildew, which will coat the fruit and leaves with a grey mould.

Strawberries: Most commercially produced strawberries are grown in vast polytunnels and are sprayed with a cocktail of fungicides, insecticides and herbicides so that they can be packaged to look glossy and uniform on the supermarket shelf. What should be a delicious treat has become tasteless factory-fruit.

The answer is to grow them yourself. Then you can have the ultimate luxury of a bowl of fresh berries still warm from the sun (chilling takes away all taste).

Strawberries grow best in really rich, moisture-retentive soil. Lots of sunshine provides a much better flavour but a shady spot will give you a later harvest.

It is best to plant in September so that they can build a good root system for the following summer. Be generous with the spacing – they are hungry, sprawling plants, so 12–18in is about right.

Strawberries are best eaten straight from the hot July soil

They need water – lots of it – when the fruits start to appear but not once they start to ripen, and preferably only to the roots as they are very prone to fungal diseases and viruses. Mulch the soil with straw to keep the fruits off the damp soil.

Blackbirds love strawberries so they must be netted from the first sign of ripening until the end of July.

They are a crop that must be constantly moved around, otherwise they build up and harbour viruses, so they should be planted into fresh soil that has not grown strawberries for four years or more. After three productive years, the plants should be dug up and composted. This means you need four strawberry plots at any one time. Never plant strawberries in a piece of ground that has grown strawberries in the previous year.

Mildew is a very common problem. Generous spacing, light and air is the best answer, along with cloches (to keep the foliage and fruit dry) if it is wet and warm, especially in June.

Alpine strawberries: Alpine strawberries have very small, dark and astonishingly intense-tasting berries that will crop continuously from midsummer through to late autumn. They are very easy to grow, enjoying rich soil and moist shade. Birds tend to leave alpine strawberries alone so netting is not essential. Plant about 12–15in apart although the best way to grow them is from seed, sown in spring.

Raspberries: There are two kinds of raspberry – summer- and autumn-fruiting. Summer raspberries fruit between the end of June and August, and autumn-fruiting ones overlap for a week or so in August and then, depending on the weather, can be picked well into October.

They like plenty of moisture, can cope with quite a lot of shade and do best in cool summers. They will grow in any soil although a slightly acidic, light, well-draining one suits them best. Before planting, it is a good idea to dig deeply, adding plenty of organic material to improve drainage and root run. Do not use mushroom compost with raspberries as it is too alkaline.

If your soil is heavy, it is a good idea to plant the roots level with the surface, mounding the soil over them, which avoids the risk of the plants standing over winter in a puddle of water. The canes should be set in the ground vertically and cut back to 9in after planting.

Summer-fruiting raspberries ripen on canes that grew the previous year whilst autumn-fruiting ones bear their berries on the current year's growth. So once autumn-fruiting ones have finished and lost their leaves, everything above ground can be cut back ready for the new, fruit-bearing growth to appear the following spring.

Do this to the summer-fruiting varieties however, and you will have no raspberries the following summer. Instead, by late August, once they stop producing berries, the old brown canes that fruited can be cut down to the ground, leaving only the new green canes standing. These can then be tied into position ready to bear next summer's crop.

This means that summer-fruiting raspberries need a permanent infrastructure that will provide constant support – thick wire strung between solid posts is the most common and effective method, but there is no reason why a trellis or fence will not do the job – whereas autumn-fruiting ones only need temporary support with canes and string, rather in the manner of broad beans.

Tayberries: These are a cross between a raspberry and a blackberry; the fruits are large, dark purple and produced from July to August. Tayberries require moist, organic-matter-rich soil and cool conditions. Severe winter weather can, however, damage plants. As with summer raspberries, cut out old canes that have fruited, leaving a space of 5in between new canes.

Blackberries: These are no longer the preserve of the wild hedgerows as thornless varieties provide gardeners with delicious fruit without any pain. Fruits appear from late July to September, and plants require soil enriched with plenty of organic matter. Prune out old canes that have fruited to encourage production of vigorous new canes.

Names

Know the names and provenance of everything. The more you can find out about who made it, where it came from, how it was made and what materials were used, the better.

Anonymity makes for easy irresponsibility. Try and personalise everything you eat, wear and use.

All those Latin names! Do not be intimidated. There has to be some universal language that determines and labels all flora, and it might as well be Latin as any other language. It is so much more important to know if a plant makes your heart sing than what its Latin name is or how often it should be watered.

Learn and celebrate vernacular names. They have a poetry and music Latin can never have. We should keep Latin for identification rather than description. One of the delights of vernacular plant names is that they vary from region to region with Celtic, Norse, Latin and Norman origins. They are meanings that grow up with the people's tongue and therefore strike directly to local experience – even if that has now become muddled into a general mess of modern life.

The best way to learn the names is to get to know the plants personally and you will find the names just stick.

And remember, nobody knows everything. Not even Roy Lancaster.

Cosmos seedlings »

The Months

Here are some jobs that I recommend you do
in your garden month by month.

January

After the closed shutters of December, it always feels to me as though the garden emerges into January – slowly, tentatively testing the waters. The gardener in me behaves in exactly the same way, gradually reacquainting myself with this cold, sodden patch of land that offers little other than the memory and promise of delight.

I like the way that the work slowly builds throughout the month, with enough impetus to take me through the coldest, dankest days, yet without any sense of urgency or pressure. It is still undeniably winter and yet the glimmers of spring are there – the snowdrop buds, perhaps a few brave aconites and, increasingly as the climate shifts, a few early primroses and violets.

But the truth remains that it is only just a gardening month. The days are short, the weather often hopelessly hostile and the chances to get anything done, sporadic and brief.

Pruning

Perhaps the biggest January job is pruning the orchard. A few afternoons spent with a pair of secateurs and a sharp saw – and the improvement in the quality of pruning saws over the past decade or so has transformed this job – gradually cutting away excess or damaged branches and encouraging the spurs that will carry next autumn's harvest, is both an enjoyable, healing process for me and an investment in the future of the garden.

Fruit trees

Woody plants such as trees and shrubs respond to pruning differently depending on whether they are actively growing or dormant.

If you prune in winter, it stimulates vigorous regrowth, not just in individual shoots but in the quantity of new shoots that appear just below and around the cut.

This means that if you remove a large branch, it will be replaced by a sprouting of multiple new shoots, and also that if a branch is growing very weakly, it can be encouraged to have renewed vigour by – counter-intuitively – cutting it back hard.

However, if you make the same cuts in July, the tree will do the exact opposite – restrict growth in direct response to your pruning. This is why trained forms such as cordons, espaliers or fans are primarily pruned in summer (see page 162).

For regular winter pruning, start by removing any crossing or rubbing branches. Cut back any overlong or straggly branches to a bud to promote vigorous multi-stemmed regrowth. A good guide is to establish a framework of permanent branches spaced widely enough so that a pigeon could fly right through them.

Most apples and pears produce their fruit on spurs – the knobbly side shoots on more mature branches. These spurs take 2–3 years to become mature enough to produce fruit, which means that any new growth will never bear any fruit in the year, and often in the two years, after winter pruning.

Do not winter prune plums, apricots, peaches or cherries (these should be pruned in late spring and only if absolutely necessary).

Trained fruit (cordons, espaliers, fans)

Remember that the harder you cut, the stronger the regrowth, so cut back any weak growth to encourage vigorous new shoots for training to the required shape in spring. But the most important pruning will be done in July (see page 239).

Soft fruit

Cut back autumn-fruiting raspberries to the ground and cut away all crossing and inward-growing growth from redcurrants and gooseberries to create an open goblet shape. Reduce remaining growth by a third to create a strong framework of branches that carry the spurs from which the fruit will form (see pages 195–199).

Bulbs

January is not too late to plant tulips but it is something that should definitely be finished by the middle of the month, or else the flowering will be noticeably late and diminished. I often pot up the latest-flowering bulbs and give them some extra protection to provoke earlier flowering but like many bulbs, tulips need a period of cold to stimulate growth, so leave the pots outside until you see the new shoots appear and then bring them into a greenhouse or porch.

At this time of year I also like to spread a layer of finished compost on any vegetable beds that are not carrying a crop so it can be worked into the soil by worms and weather, ready for sowing and planting in a few months' time. Finally, a January job is to sieve compost and bag it up to add to potting compost, ready for the flurry of sowing in spring.

Chillies

Chillies need a long growing season so they can become strong enough by early summer to develop their flowers. The bigger the plant, the more fruits you will have and to get a decent-sized plant, you need to start it early. I like to start sowing chilli seeds at the end of January, with a second sowing in late February or early March. I scatter the seeds thinly on a seed tray of peat-free compost and put them on a heated bench to germinate – which they do very slowly, so do not worry if nothing seems to be happening for a few weeks. They do need warmth to germinate so if you do not have a heated mat, a windowsill above a radiator will do the job.

February

I remember that my mother hated February most of all the months. Winter had gone on too long and spring seemed too far. For her, its only saving grace was that it was the shortest of the months. I know others share that view but I like February. I like the way that it opens out and releases the valves for spring. I like the way that the days reach out, stretching, limbering up.

February is the month of small but powerful things. Catkins, snowdrops, aconites, crocus, hellebores, violets, primroses – all resist snow, ice and scything east winds to blaze with jewel-like intensity. There is something entirely hopeful and brave about these harbingers of spring that fills me full of cheer and whets my horticultural edge. If they can feel spring round the corner, then so can I.

There is all the pruning to finish by the end of the month and any bare-root planting, too – if the ground allows. If it is not too wet or too frozen, I will try and complete the mulching of the borders as well. Whereas up to Christmas I have a strong sense of laying the garden to rest for winter, all February work is about setting things ready for what is to come. It feels like the preparations for a party.

Bare-root plants

Most people buy all their plants in a container from a garden centre. But woody plants such as trees and shrubs of all kinds can be bought 'bare-root'. This means that they are raised in the ground and only lifted just before delivery. They will arrive with the roots wrapped in a bag of some kind but with no soil around them. I always try and buy bare-root trees and shrubs if I can.

The advantages of bare-root plants are that they are invariably cheaper, usually better quality and there is always a wider range of types and varieties of bare-root plants to choose from as opposed to containerised ones. They also are more likely to get established and grow more quickly in your garden than container-grown plants.

The only disadvantage is that, unlike a tree in a pot, you cannot put them to one side and plant them whenever you have the time or inclination. As soon as they arrive, they should be placed in a bucket of water for an hour to give them a drink. Then either plant them immediately, taking them straight from the water to the planting hole so the roots do not dry out even for an instant, or heel them in until you are ready.

'Heeling in' means digging a trench or hole in a spare piece of soil (usually the veg patch) and, without any of the finesse of actual planting, burying the roots to protect them. It is best to put trees in at 45 degrees so they are not rocked by wind. If you have bought a number of hedging plants or young trees, they will come in a bundle. This should be untied and the plants placed individually but closely spaced so the roots do not get entangled as they grow if they are left for a while (and I have left such plants heeled in for more than a year with no apparent ill-effects).

Veg

Leave potatoes at this time of year in the dark and they start to sprout long, translucent, brittle shoots. But put them in a frost-free brightly lit place, and they slowly develop knobbly green or purple shoots, which are ready to grow quickly when placed in the soil. This process is called 'chitting'.

Whilst chitting is not necessary for maincrop varieties, First or Second earlies benefit from being chitted by being ready to harvest at least a week if not two weeks earlier than those planted unchitted – and an early harvest is always desirable for new potatoes and has the advantage of increasing the opportunities to lift the tubers before the risk of blight.

Put the seed potatoes in a tray or egg box, placing each potato upright to encourage a tuber to grow from the end. Place them in a sunny, frost-free place such as a cool windowsill for 4–8 weeks so that when you are ready to plant them – usually around Easter – they will grow away fast.

Ideally, onion and shallot 'sets' (small bulbs) should be planted out as early as possible in the year but in my garden, the ground is invariably too wet and cold and they will not grow until the soil warms up. So I always start them in plugs, sitting the sets almost on the surface of the compost and putting them in the greenhouse where they will steadily grow, developing strong foliage and a good root system.

These can be gradually hardened off before planting out when the soil is ready. The only thing to watch is that the roots do not outgrow the available space. As the plants grow, gently lift a random seedling and check that the roots are not becoming crowded. You should be able to hold the plant by its stem and the compost should be clearly visible, but held as a neat plug by the roots.

The increasing light levels in February mean that salad crops planted in a greenhouse in autumn offer a generous supply of fresh leaves every day. Rocket, mizuna and lettuces like 'Winter Density' and 'Rouge d'Hiver' all survive the winter with a little protection (I always grow them in an unheated greenhouse) and then start to grow very strongly.

I sow another batch of seed in early February, which will be ready to replace this batch of plants in mid-March.

Ideally, onion and shallot sets should be planted out as early as possible in the year

At the same time, I sow broad beans under cover in pots or root trainers so they can be planted out into a raised bed as healthy plants in early April.

Raised beds do (or should) not need digging in winter but a top-dressing of an inch or two of garden compost spread over them will incorporate into the soil over the coming month or so whilst the soil warms up sufficiently to sow direct.

Pruning

By mid-February all the late winter/early spring pruning of climbers and shrubs can begin and continue until the middle of March. I practise this, focussing mainly on the roses, clematis and shrubs such as buddleia.

....

Roses

There is no mystery to pruning roses and there is practically nothing you can do that the plant will not recover from. So relax and enjoy it! The only rules are to use sharp secateurs or loppers so the cuts are never forced, and to try and cut just above a bud or leaf – and don't worry if it is outward-facing or not. Any bud will do.

First remove all damaged or crossing stems. Then cut back hard any stems that look too weak to support their own weight. Finally, remove any old, woody stems that are crowding the shrub by cutting right down to their base. Most Shrub roses do not need any other pruning but can be reduced by a third to encourage early budding and a more compact shape. Hybrid Teas, Floribundas and China roses follow the same sort of remedial treatment and then have all remaining healthy shoots cut back by two-thirds to leave a basic framework from which the new, flowering, shoots will grow.

> # There is no mystery to pruning roses and there is practically nothing you can do that the plant will not recover from

Climbing roses should be pruned to maintain a framework of long stems trained as laterally as possible, with side branches breaking vertically all the way along them. These side branches will carry the flowers on new growth produced in spring, so can all be pruned back to a healthy bud – leaving no more than a couple of inches of growth.

Ramblers differ from climbers, which tend to have large flowers,

often appearing more than once in the summer and on some, continuously for months, whereas ramblers have clusters of smaller flowers that invariably flower just once in midsummer. These include 'Bobbie James', 'Rambling Rector' and 'Paul's Himalayan Musk'. These need little pruning at all and never in winter or spring as the flowers are carried mostly on stems grown in late summer. Any pruning to train or restrict them should be done immediately after flowering.

Clematis

The simplest rule is, 'If it flowers before June, do not prune'. So for early flowerers like *Clematis montana*, *C. alpina* or *C. armandii*, do not prune at all save to tidy their sprawl after they have finished flowering. Clematis with large flowers like 'Marie Boisselot' or 'Nelly Moser' should be cut back by about a third and for late-flowering clematis (i.e. flowering after midsummer's day, 24 June) such as *C. viticella*, prune all top growth – the whole caboodle – in late winter right down to 6–12in from the ground, leaving just two healthy buds.

And if you are not sure what your clematis is (or whether your rose is a climber or a rambler), then leave it, let it flower and make a note for next year.

Shrubs

Spring-flowering shrubs such as philadelphus, deutzia, weigela and rubus all produce their flowers on shoots grown the previous summer so should not be pruned until after they have finished flowering.

However, shrubs such as buddleia, cornus, salix, spiraea, deciduous ceanothus and *Fuchsia fulgens* and *F. magellanica*, all flower on new wood, so can be cut hard back very hard just like late-flowering clematis. The harder they are cut, the more they will flower.

Cutting back grasses

Almost all border grasses look splendid throughout winter but they are beginning to look tired by mid-February. Deciduous grasses like miscanthus, calamagrostis and deschampsia should all be cut back hard to the ground before the new green shoots appear. This is because you do not want to reduce this year's fresh shoots but only reduce last year's old growth. However, evergreen grasses like the stipa and cortaderia families should have their old growth removed by combing through each plant with a rake or your hands (I advise wearing stout gloves as grasses can be very sharp). However, do not divide or move any grasses at this time of year. They must be growing strongly to have the best chance of surviving, so wait until mid- or even late spring to do this.

March

If February is lit by anticipation, March is the month when things start to happen. The hawthorn hedges start to prickle with fresh green leaves and the snowdrops are replaced with a great flush of daffodils, crocus, hellebores and even the first species tulips. The game has begun. By the last week of the month, the days are longer than the nights and the clocks shift into summer time, giving gardeners the gift of an extra hour when they can most use it. But March is never without a sting in its tail. The weather can be capricious, ranging from warm drought to snow and gales – sometimes on the same day – so do not be lulled into an over-eager false sense of security. Although all instinct is to make as much headway as possible, it is better to be a bit late in spring rather than early.

But the signs of life are irrepressible, from the dawn chorus to the buds on the hawthorns and the daffodils, with crocus and fritillaries flowering freely. And the itch to get outside grows more urgent by the day regardless of the weather. There is housekeeping to be done, – supports, ties, repairs and preparations, – all reconnecting gardener to garden and guiding you both into the arms of spring.

My favourite spring flowers are our native primroses. With their tussocks of pale yellow flowers tucked under hedgerows and shrubs, flowering with their particular bright delicacy despite being battered by wind and rain and collared by a ruff of snow, they seem to capture all the hope and innocence of a brave new spring.

One of my breakfast treats at this time of year is the first stewed rhubarb with yoghurt. No combination has a cleaner, sharper and yet hauntingly sweet taste that is guaranteed to brighten the sleepiest head and set you up for the rigours of the day ahead.

I grow a number of different varieties of rhubarb that provide a staggered harvest from the first fragile shoots that we pick to eat at Christmas to the last harvest at the beginning of July. Early and extra sweet rhubarb can be forced by excluding all light from the plant. This suppresses leaf growth down to a yellow flame at the end of a long pale pink stem whose sugars are greatly increased as a result. I tend to use 'Timperly Early' for this early harvest and it is, as the name suggests, an excellent early forcing variety.

All herbaceous plants and deciduous trees and shrubs can be planted in March if the ground is not too wet, but for trees and shrubs in particular, this should be done by the end of the month. Evergreens, however, can safely wait until April. When planting any woody tree or shrub, the soil should be dug out in a wide but not deep hole, and loosened to encourage a free root run but not enriched directly beneath the plant. This will encourage it to spread its roots quickly. However, everything should receive a generous mulch of compost on top of the soil after it has been watered in.

When planting any woody tree or shrub, the soil should be dug out in a wide but not deep hole

Any winter pruning can be completed and shrubs with especially decorative bark, such as cornus, willow and sambucus, can also be cut back hard to encourage fresh shoots whose bark will glow with extra bright colour next winter.

In mid-March I take the dahlia tubers out from their winter storage, go through them all to remove any that have dried up or rotted, and then pot them all up. A few will be put onto the hot bench to provide shoots for cuttings but the rest go into a cold frame to gently start their journey into spring growth so that when they can be planted out after the last frost (not before mid-May here), they are growing strongly.

March is the time to sow many seeds and get the whole propagation process going. Hardy and tender vegetables, herbs, tender flowering annuals and herbaceous perennials can all be sown in March if you have space and protection for them.

This is where cold frames are invaluable. In fact in spring, I would rather forgo my greenhouses than the cold frames. They offer enough protection to keep the tenderest seedling from the harshest weather and yet can be opened right out to start the essential hardening-off process. And as the month progresses, my cold frames are the real measure of progress, regardless of how bare the garden might be.

It is a good idea to check all support for climbers before they start to put on too much growth. This might be wires and strainers attached to a wall or fence, or tripods made from bean sticks. Replace any that are not strong and retie the remainder.

Mulch

March is made for mulch – a layer spread over the surface of the soil. It generally refers to organic material like garden compost, woodchips, bark or cocoa shells, but can equally consist of gravel or slate chips.

There is a two- or three-week window between the new herbaceous and bulb growth starting to show thinly in the borders and the point when the new growth becomes too thick to conveniently work around. It is in this period that mulching is best done.

Mulching in spring with any organic layer serves as a soil conditioner, weed-suppressant and moisture retainer. Individually, all three are important but combined, they make a radical difference to your borders and your time. An effective mulch means little or no weeding, little or no watering and an improved soil that will make for much healthier plants.

A mulch controls weeds by denying them light. A minimum depth of 2in is a good rule of thumb, with 4in probably being an ideal. With annual weeds like goosegrass, chickweed and groundsel (that can grow and set seed within an amazing five weeks), emerging seedlings will not develop and the seeds will not germinate. Perennial weeds will grow through a mulch but weakly, and are much easier to pull up as a result.

Do not skimp on the thickness simply to make your mulch go round. It is better to do half an area properly than the whole thing too thinly. Avoid smothering the crowns of perennials and go around groups of annual seedlings if necessary. Most bulbs will push through but any well-grown leaves of daffodils or tulips should be allowed to stick through it.

A mulch will be worked into the soil over the course of a year (about six months for garden compost and a full year or more for bark chippings). Very light soil is given more body and very heavy soil opened out.

It makes sense to do all the border 'housework' such as weeding, dividing and moving plants, and adding any new perennials or shrubs before you mulch so that the mulch is disturbed as little as possible once you have spread it.

April

Of all the months, this is the one where the world changes most dramatically from the first day to the last. April Fool's day is clearly spring but tentatively so, but the 30th is filled with green and blossom, and radiant with tulips, wallflowers, hawthorn, cow parsley and clematis. The whole world seems to be exploding into flower.

The month opens with a prickle of green in the hedgerows and ends full-blown, steaming into May on a fanfare of new growth. It is the month of daffodils and, most gloriously, of tulips, rising to their crescendo here in the last week of the month, a brilliantly gaudy St George's Day celebration.

Although the garden is filling with early clematis, bulbs, spring perennials and the blossom making the orchard trees seem as though they are floating in a floral cloud, it is really the growth of green that makes April unlike any other month. At the beginning, the garden is still dominated by bare brown branches and empty brown soil, but four weeks later it is flushed with green of the most vibrant, life-infused kind and all other colours are set and measured against this.

And if the burgeoning of the garden was not delight enough, April is blessed by the return of the swallows and martins. They bring with them a great surge of happiness and a sense that now spring can really begin.

These first outliers, arriving in dribs and drabs, exhausted and half-starved from their epic journey from South Africa, return now to within a few hundred yards of where they were born, bobbing and roller-coasting in the sky for the first few weeks and then, as they gain strength and begin the urgent business of nesting and raising at least two and often three broods, scything the garden sky into arabesques.

Here we have had a pair of swallows nesting in exactly the same spot each year in one of our sheds for the past 25 years. They are voracious feeders, swooping in and out of the nest hundreds of times a day, eating flies and thousands of aphids, so they are good friends to the gardener.

They are also an excellent guide to the weather, because they follow the insects which, in turn, rise and fall according to the air pressure. This means that when the swallows are soaring high, there is a good chance of fine weather the next day, and when they are swooping just inches from the ground to pluck insects with astonishing dexterity, the pressure is low and it is likely that rain will follow.

Tulips

When the tulips hit their April stride, the year turns a corner. Early spring breaks into a range of delicate and often subtle colours tempered by green until tulips burst onto this muted palette with a fanfare of every colour except blue (there is a 'Blue Parrot' tulip but its shade of blue is at best an approximation). They are the first real blaze of colour of the year and are the most silkily sensuous of all flowers.

As with all bulbs, do not cut tulip leaves back after flowering as they are needed to feed and create the new bulb for next year's flowers. However, the seedhead should be snapped off so none of the bulb's energy is spent in making seed. The whole plant, bulb, leaves and all, can be dug up and stored in racks in a dry, sunny place or replanted in a nursery bed. When the leaves have died back naturally, the bulbs can be stored in a dry shed until autumn.

> As with all bulbs, do not cut tulip leaves back after flowering as they are needed to feed and create the new bulb for next year's flowers

Most tulips will only produce one good flowering bulb each year together with a number of smaller bulbils. These may take a few years to develop a bulb big enough to flower, which is why tulips left in the ground tend to get smaller and more numerous each year. It is best to top up the display with some fresh bulbs each November.

Veg

I don't think that anything makes me happier than an April evening spent preparing the ground and sowing veg seeds for a summer harvest whilst the garden settles gradually around me. All winter the ground lies cold and wet, but when that clammy chill in the hand is replaced by warmth, and as the soil responds to the caress of a rake preparing a tilth, it is as though I am returned to the rightful earth.

Some plants have evolved to thrive in cool (but not cold) weather and rocket is one of these. It is at its most peppery, buttery best in April from seeds sown in late January and planted outside in March, and does well again from an August sowing to harvest in autumn. It makes a particularly useful catch crop in ground intended for any vegetable that is not fully hardy but which thrives in rich soil and is normally planted out towards the end of May.

Splitting hostas

Whilst I love the sheer luxuriance of growth of the really large hostas like *Hosta* 'Snowden', *H. sieboldiana* or *H.* 'Sum and Substance', they can quickly get very large and crowd out neighbouring plants, and need regular division. This not only makes some space around them but also reinvigorates the hosta and creates a number of new plants. The perfect time to do this is just as they start to show vigorous growth in April.

I find the best way is to dig up the entire plant and place it, roots and all, on top of the soil. Then smaller plants can be created by chopping it into segments like a cake with a sharp spade. This means that each piece will mainly consist of the outer part of the plant, which is newer and more vigorous than the older, less productive core. These wedges can then be replanted either singly or in a couple of new groups.

With really large, more established plants, it is often easier to divide them with a saw. Place the plant on a table and saw it into segments, composting any of the really woody heart. Always give the replanted sections a thorough soak after replanting and mulch them thickly with good garden compost.

Taking pelargonium cuttings

As pelargoniums put on new growth in spring, it is a good idea to both cut them back to shape and to use this material for cuttings to make fresh plants. Strip off the lower leaves of the cuttings and make a clean cut across the stems with a sharp knife. Insert up to four cuttings into a pot of very gritty, free-draining compost. Some, like the Angel pelargoniums, take very easily. However, they are prone to rotting off if they become too humid, so do not put the cuttings in a polythene bag or propagator but water them and then put them somewhere warm (ideally on a heated mat). Keep the cuttings dry and the compost moist. You will know when they have taken when you see new growth.

Hardening off

Hardening off is essential for any plant that has been raised under protection, whether it be in a greenhouse, cold frame or windowsill. It is especially important in spring, when the weather can fluctuate dramatically.

Ideally, hardening off is done in stages over a couple of weeks via a succession of increasingly exposed but controlled environments. So a heated greenhouse is followed by an unheated cold frame that can be closed at night and then, after a week or so, the plant is put outside in a spot sheltered from cold winds or harsh sunshine. This allows it to acclimatise and adapt to variations in weather and temperature before being finally planted into its growing position. And, as a result, it will grow much faster and healthier than if thrust from a cosseted environment into the brutal realities of outdoor weather.

In practice, most people do not have these resources but it is definitely worth creating a sheltered spot near the house or shed that is a protected holding bay for young plants.

May

A beautiful garden in May is the very best that life can offer. It is like falling in love. All lyric poetry, all mystical expression, all the sublimest music strain towards what every leaf does as carelessly each spring as when it falls in autumn. May is a bit like Christmas. Every day feels like a celebration. All the rituals and signs are familiar and predictable and yet May never fails to thrill and excite me. Bluebells, apple blossom, cow parsley, irises, the early species roses, aquilegias, alliums and oriental poppies are all greeted as long-lost friends even as they delight me with all the freshness of discovery.

But the very best thing about May is not the flowers but the astonishing range and intensity of greens that unfurl throughout the month. It is like watching a wonderful sunset. They cannot be captured or held, so the only sane thing to do is to immerse yourself in them and relish every rich, disappearing second.

It can be cold – it is a rare May when we do not have some frost and I have even known it to snow. It is often wet, occasionally parched, and grey skies are more or less guaranteed. No matter. The sheer radiance of the garden, the energy that cannot be suppressed or diminished, rides over any weather and fills the garden with a constant, soaring song of delight.

Supporting perennials

The one cliché about supporting plants is to do it before the plant needs it. The thinking behind this is twofold. To start with, if you place supports in position whilst the plants are still relatively short, they will quickly be hidden by the new growth and as a result your borders will not look corseted and constrained. The second reason is that any plant that has been knocked or collapsed never looks the same, however carefully you prop it up. So for the sake of naturalness and as an effective support, I like to keep twiggy prunings – hazel is ideal – which are free, biodegradable yet strong, easy to push into the soil and hold tender new growth firmly without damaging it or forcing it to lose its natural form.

Everything starts to grow fast in May – including weeds. The only answer is to try and keep on top of them so they do not become a major job. Some plants – like onions and garlic – are very sensitive to competition and should be regularly hoed off so the weeds never get a chance to rob them of available moisture and nutrition. Regular hoeing when the weeds are very small is the best way. A sharp hoe in dry soil makes very light work of this, cutting off the weed roots just below the surface of the soil. If you always hoe in the morning on a dry day, the weeds will dry out in the sun and die, whereas hoeing on a damp day or in the evening runs the risk of plants that have not been fully chopped off surviving and regrowing.

The only answer to weeds is to try and keep on top of them so they do not become a major job

Once we reach the middle of May it is reasonable to put out the tender plants that have needed protection from frost for the past seven months or so. In my case this amounts to bananas, cannas, dahlias, tree dahlias, oranges and lemons, agapanthus, salvias, cosmos, pelargoniums, aeoniums, lemon verbenas, French tarragon and various lavenders and fuchsias – all crammed into every spare bit of heated space for months on end and longing to get out into sunlight.

But it is important to harden them off gradually, exposing them to cool air by degrees and having some protection if there is a late frost, either by covering them with fleece or bringing them back under cover.

What really changes things is the combination of lengthening days and hotter nights. I always plant my tomatoes into position in the middle of the month – around Chelsea week – and plant out tender annuals like zinnias, tithonias and sunflowers into the borders,

knowing that all these plants will start to really surge into growth rather than hunker under the spring cold.

Then, when they are all in place, the garden takes on a cosmopolitan, jaunty air and becomes a catwalk, strutting its stuff with a flounce. What is lost in modesty is gained with a new panache.

....

Asparagus

Although you can now buy fresh asparagus most days of the year, May and June are its true season. Asparagus takes up space, needs special conditions and is only harvestable from May to July. But home-grown asparagus is a true treat and no asparagus bought out of season is anything like as good as spears cut from your garden and rushed straight to the boiling pan of water. Like new potatoes, peas or sweetcorn, asparagus is one of those harvests that diminishes in quality after harvesting almost by the minute.

Traditionally it does best in sandy soil but it grows well on any fertile ground. If your soil is on the heavy side, it needs to be grown on a ridge to keep the plants up out of wet soil. Drainage is the key, however that is achieved. You can plant them on a ridge made at the bottom of a trench, draping the roots either side of the ridge and then mounding soil up over them. Or simply add lots of grit to your soil and plant the crowns 6–9in deep, straight into the ground. But either way, do not compromise on the drainage.

June

June enters into the garden with the last vestiges of spring clinging to it and ends in high summer with the first cut of long grass, roses in their prime and the garden as ripe as a plum. The whole month is a swelling crescendo, filled with long, lovely days when you can come home after a full day's work and go outside for hours longer. My idea of horticultural heaven is to be weeding or planting as the light gently falls around me, and to be able to continue with light enough to work until after 10pm.

I carry these few precious evenings with me for the rest of the year rather like a pebble in my pocket that I can touch, and they see me through the dark days of winter. Whilst many would relish sitting watching the garden gently fade into the summer night, half the pleasure for me is that there is so much to do. The vegetable garden needs constant attention from sowing to harvest, and the borders need the reinjection of tender annuals that will carry on the season once the early summer flush has passed. I sow a lot of seeds throughout the month and take as many cuttings as I can, tapping into the energy of this high point of the year to carry it into future seasons.

My idea of horticultural heaven is to be weeding or planting as the light gently falls around me

I always feel that June answers questions that the rest of the year poses. Some are practical – how will this border look at its very best? How sunny will this corner be at the peak of the year? Where does the sun rise on the longest day? But some are philosophical. Why do I garden? How does such a small patch of this earth give me so very much pleasure? Answers clearly to be found at every corner of a June garden.

But so much is still promised that the fact that the garden is brimming over with beauty and sensual delight does not bring the slightest pang of regret or incipient loss in the way that August days do, with autumn just glimpsed around the corner of a late summer's day. Everything still has the freshness and inner glow. Nothing is jaded. Nothing has yet been taken for granted.

In the vegetable garden, now is the time to sow and plant the tender vegetables such as squashes, French beans, sweetcorn, chicories, tomatoes and peppers. In the borders, the northern long-day plants peak and dominate with their generally gentle fulsomeness, whilst the tender short-day plants from nearer the equator move up to take their place, richer, sleeker and ready to dominate high summer.

Species roses

I love roses of all kinds and in June my garden is blessed with the blooms of hundreds of them. I adore the classic or old-fashioned roses – Gallicas, Damasks, Bourbons, Albas, Centifolias, etc., all with romantic and evocative names – that flower only once and then just for a month or so, but do so in such a manner as to spread their beauty right through the year. But they are easy to love.

> ## I love roses of all kinds and in June my garden is blessed with the blooms of hundreds of them

Much less well appreciated are the species roses. These are plants only ever known by their formal Latin titles, devoid of the intimacy of hybrid names, yet as charming and elegant as anything a garden can grow.

We have come to think of the most desirable roses as having large flower heads or perhaps a mass of convoluted petals, but all species roses have much simpler flower forms and are often really quite small. However, the massed effect of their display can be breathtaking and

their simplicity adds almost an innocence that you rarely find in man-made hybrids.

Species roses occur naturally without variation, and unlike roses that are grafted – which includes every single named variety – will come true from seed when pollinated by themselves or others of the same species. The hand of man has never improved them. If they tangle and twist, then that is what they do. If they only flower for a few days, then that is unchangeable. This imbues them with a freshness and wildness that I love – and they hardly ever suffer from any of the afflictions of their more highly bred cousins.

Tender plants

All through April and May we have been growing on, nurturing, protecting and increasingly hardening off tender plants such as cannas, dahlias and salvias, as well as tender annuals like tithonias, cosmos and zinnias, all of which play such an important role in the late-summer borders. By June we can plant them out with confidence that they will not only be free from any risk of frost, but also that the nights will be warm enough for them to grow strongly and establish as good-sized plants ready for their flowering display.

Inevitably there are trays of plants that were sown too early and are consequently outgrowing their containers. Whilst they relish the new-found nourishment and freedom of a border, they never quite do as well as those that are planted out at the critical period when they are still healthy in their plug or pot but are perfectly ready to grow out into the soil. I reckon that this happens with most plants grown from seed during a period that is as short as 10 days. Timing is everything.

Having watered them in well, these tender plants are actually quite able to cope with any British summer weather and can be left unwatered and unfed for the rest of the summer to encourage the roots to spread and find the goodness they need as widely and as deeply as possible.

Artichokes

Artichokes are one of the few vegetables (along with ruby chard, purple kale and climbing beans) that are truly worth their place in a border as well as producing delicious food. They do best in full sun and rich soil although they need good drainage. A generous addition of compost in the planting hole deals with both requirements. It is best to be patient and remove any flower stems in the first year, allowing all the growing energy to go into the roots and leaves. Then in the second year, they should grow with much more vigour and produce at least two cuttings of chokes. Although they are perennials and can live for many years, after their third year of maturity (fourth year from seed) the plants become less productive.

> # Artichokes are one of the few vegetables that are truly worth their place in a border as well as producing delicious food

But if you take offsets from the second year onwards, you will have a constant supply of second- and third-year plants, which produce the best harvest. For an offset, simply chop off a piece of root in spring, with a slither of leaf attached from the parent, and plant it where it is to grow. Do not worry when the leaf shrivels and dies as new leaves will take its place. Leave it to establish for the first year, mulch it thickly to protect against frost, and it will really take off in its second spring.

Pruning

Spring-flowering shrubs and climbers such as *Clematis montana* or *C. alpina*, and shrubs like lilac, philadelphus or ribes, can be pruned at the beginning of the month when all flowering has finished. Clematis can be trimmed with shears to reduce sprawl or – every few years – cut back hard to stimulate fresh, less untidy growth. The resulting new growth made over the rest of summer will carry next year's flowers.

Shrubs like lilac should have their oldest shoots removed right to the base, taking out no more than a third of the plant at any one time. Remove any crossing or damaged growth and finish by making sure that they are weeded and mulched well to encourage healthy new shoots.

A tip: I always go round the garden in early June trimming the vertical edges of the hedges flanking entrances and exits. This is by no means a proper hedge-cut – which should not be done now because it would disturb nesting birds – but a very light trim. It is amazing how this tightens and adds crispness to the entire garden.

July

My birthday falls in July so there is always an element of a new year as we enter that month. There is some objective evidence of this – the days are becoming shorter and plants are reacting accordingly. The nights are getting warmer and the sense of summer being borrowed from spring that you inevitably have in at least the first part of June, is gone. Summer has become a stately galleon sailing fully rigged regardless of the daily vagaries of the weather.

Cannas, dahlias, sunflowers, cosmos – all flex their muscles. The sweet peas are at their glorious best and for the first half of the month, the roses are radiant. The vegetable garden is starting to really bear forth with peas, beans, salad crops, new potatoes, beetroot, garlic, carrots and artichokes all demanding harvest.

The garden is ripe and rich like a plum ready to be plucked from the tree. This is its hour and should be relished, and yet a slight shadow of melancholy is caught in the corner of my eye. The days start to shrink. That youthful, irrepressible freshness of June cannot be recreated. Something infinitely precious has gone and with it – always – the overriding sense of not having paid enough attention, of not having valued each moment with the rapture that it surely deserved.

The garden is ripe and rich like a plum ready to be plucked from the tree

Borders enter a completely new phase in July with the tender, short-day plants such as all the tender annuals, salvias, dahlias and cannas replacing oriental poppies, delphiniums and irises, and space has to be made – sometimes ruthlessly – to accommodate them. The least painful way to do this is to remove early annuals and biennials such as

forget-me-nots, wallflowers and, as they finish towards the end of the month, foxgloves.

As the first flush of roses starts to fade, it makes a huge difference if you deadhead regularly – even daily. This will stimulate the development of side shoots with further flowering buds, and is a pruning rather than a tidying process, so should be done with secateurs. Do not just take off the spent petals but cut back to a leaf or side shoot, removing as much stem as is necessary.

Attentive gardeners will have staked their herbaceous perennials back in May or early June, following the advice of doing so before the plant needs it. But I find that there is often another round of staking that has to follow in July.

The extra warmth of July – and the wetness that comes with it – often leads to a flush of lush growth that plants cannot support. The result is that borders can start to fall all over the place, plants outgrowing themselves and toppling chaotically – especially if lashed by rain winds or thunderstorms – and what was lovely profusion can become a disaster zone overnight.

So it is good to have some brushwood such as hazel pea sticks or metal supports ready, and to gently work round the borders, easing plants upright and providing the underpinning that they need – but without reducing them to a stiffly corsetted state. Ideally, when you have finished carefully supporting, buttressing and bolstering the border, it should look as though you have not done anything at all.

Veg

First of all are the new potatoes, emerging white and surprisingly gleaming from the soil, almost blinking in the sunlight. No potatoes ever taste as good as this first shy crop of the year. Next is the garlic crop that has been growing since October. I harvest ours when the leaves start to fade and incline to set a minaret of seed, lifting them carefully with a fork so as not to damage the necks before drying them in the sun for a few weeks so that they will store through to the following spring. Beans, peas, the first tomatoes, all the salad crops of course –

tumble from garden to kitchen with an increasing flow. It makes supermarket shopping seem a drab, dreary process.

....

Tomatoes

July is the month when greenhouse tomatoes set most fruit. Ripening is very variable but in most years we start to harvest by the end of the month. I am constantly keeping a watch on the ventilation and temperature – both controlled only by opening and closing the doors and windows. Tomatoes grow best with an even temperature and it is better to have a steady, slightly cooler heat than great fluctuations between day and night, which will manifest itself by the leaves starting to curl inwards.

I tie the growing cordons weekly, pinching out all side shoots as I go. All tomatoes develop shoots growing diagonally between the stem and leaves. These side shoots will develop fruit but have more vigour than the purely lateral fruit trusses and when growing cordons, they tend to take a large share of the plant's goodness if left unchecked. By pinching them out as they appear, you concentrate the plants' energy into producing maximum fruit.

Bush (or determinate) varieties are, as the name suggests, left to grow naturally and are often smothered in fruits for a relatively short harvesting period. But they take up a great deal more space so most people grow cordon varieties, which means you can raise both many more plants and also have a much longer, more staggered harvest.

It is important to keep a steady supply of moisture and not let your tomatoes get too wet or too dry. I find that a good soak twice a week works well for tomatoes planted in soil with plenty of organic matter. Containers will need watering every other day or even daily if it is very hot. However it is essential that any containers, including gro-bags, have good drainage so the roots do not become waterlogged. By the end of the month, as the fruits grow and start to ripen, I reduce the water so that the sugars will not be too diluted, resulting in a big but insipid tomato.

If the weather is wet and warm, the major worry is blight. Not enough ventilation and the plants remain too moist and foster the fungus. Too much and they become stressed and more vulnerable, as well as allowing more ingress to the airborne spores. The best solution is to water well just once a week and adjust the ventilation to any changes in the weather.

....

Summer pruning of fruit

Apples and pears will have put on a lot of new growth over the past three months, none of which will bear fruit for a year or two. Whereas pruning in winter stimulates renewed vigour in subsequent regrowth, summer pruning reduces vigour so is useful for curtailing over-long shoots or indeed the overall size of a tree or bush. This is especially important with trained trees such as espaliers or cordons. Cutting back now allows light and air onto the fruit that is ripening and stops your trees becoming too crowded with unproductive branches. Remove all this year's growth back to a couple of pairs of leaves (usually about 2–4in), being careful not to remove any ripening fruits.

If you are training the fruit to a particular shape, tie desired but loose growth in as you go. But if you are training espaliers with a series of parallel horizontal branches, always leave the final 6in of the growing tip untied until it has reached its desired length, when it can then be securely tied in. This is because shoots always grow much more strongly if they are allowed to grow upwards, so training them to the horizontal from the outset will slow their growth dramatically.

August

August is the month of school holidays – the rhythm of which stay with you all your life, with that bittersweet combination of long summer days and a real sense of summer slipping away. August evenings are velvet-rich with golden light as the days draw in, and the month has a fullness that pervades the whole garden. The August borders take on a kind of muscular energy, and what they lose in early-summer freshness, they gain in mature assurance.

The sun is lower in the sky and the evenings, by the end of the month, much shorter, so my favourite time of day is when the early evening sun hits the rich colours in the borders so that they glow with regal intensity.

Crocosmias, dahlias, buddleias, the late-flowering clematis, cosmos, zinnias, tithonias, sunflowers, rudbeckias, heleniums, kniphofias and salvias all compete for finery in the jewel-garden borders, all seizing August as their shining hour.

By mid-August quite a few of the early summer-flowering plants can be lifted, divided and moved so that they establish strong, healthy roots before winter dormancy, so as well as being beautiful, it can be a busy time in the flower borders, too.

By August, the sweet peas are developing new flowers weekly and unless cut regularly, these quickly set seed and that, in turn, inhibits further flowering. To extend the season, I have found it is best to cut all but the tightest buds every 10 days, and to check for and remove any seed pods daily.

Veg

August is really the peak of the vegetable year. Although the early vegetables – broad beans, spinach, radish, rocket, peas, spring cabbage – are now done, the roster of their replacements is as rich as the flowers in the border. Ruby chard, purple- and yellow-podded beans, sweetcorn, squashes, courgettes, beetroot, chicory, tomatoes, peppers, cucumbers, aubergines, Florence fennel, onions and garlic are all jostling for prize place. There is room for all of them and more in even a modest plot. Rotation, succession and a bit of planning puts a quart of summer vegetables into a pint of back garden.

August is the month of harvest. Gradually, one by one, all the crops are gathered in, from the glut of tomatoes – perfect for freezing for sauce deep into winter – to that first ripe corn on the cob or my favourite August dish, a ratatouille made from my own onions, garlic, courgettes, tomatoes, dwarf beans and chilli.

August is really the peak of the vegetable year

Amidst this cornucopia, August is also a busy month of sowing in readiness for winter and even for next spring. I sow lettuce, rocket, spring cabbages, parsley and winter onions by mid-month so that they can establish a decent root system before the fading light halts their growth.

As soon as the lowest truss of fruits form on my tomato plants, I remove all foliage beneath them. Thereafter, leaves can be regularly removed, working up the plant as the fruits form. This increases ventilation, allows more light to reach the fruits to help ripen them, and reduces the rate of the plant's growth, which in turn improves and speeds up ripening. If blight or mosaic virus strikes, you can completely defoliate the plants without harming the fruits that are growing and ripening, as the stem has enough chlorophyll to continue photosynthesis for months.

Ponds

Even a seemingly wholly natural wildlife pond needs a little maintenance throughout the year and there are a number of things to keep an eye on towards the end of summer. The first is to keep the water levels topped up, especially in dry weather. Ideally this is done with stored rainwater but if you do not have enough, then it is better to add a little tap water every day than a large amount in one go every now and then. Any foliage that has fallen in the pond should be regularly removed, along with faded and dying water-lily leaves, cutting them off with a sharp knife, not least to stop them obscuring emerging flowers.

If you are going away on holiday, any fish will be perfectly able to look after themselves, but do be sure to top the water up fully before you leave.

Oxygenating plants can increase at an alarming rate in the warm August water and need thinning out, otherwise they choke the surface and their decomposing plant material enriches the sediment too much. This encourages algal growth, which in turn creates the opaque green surface that obscures all underwater activity but that contributes so much fascination to any pond. I use a wire rake to gently comb algae and excess oxygenators from the surface of the water. Be sure to gently put the accumulated material at the edge of the pond and leave it for 24 hours before taking it to the compost heap, so all assorted wildlife in it can crawl back into the water.

Strawberries

After the early strawberries finish fruiting – usually the middle of July – they put their energy into producing new plants via runners. These are long shoots with one or more plantlets spaced along their length. As the plantlets touch the soil, they quickly put down roots. Pin the plantlets nearest to the parents (these will always be the strongest along any one runner) to the soil or onto a pot with compost in it, and leave them to establish strong roots for a few weeks before separating them from the mother plants. The resulting baby plants will have more vigour than the parents and keep your stock replenished and refreshed. I compost the parent plants after four years as their productivity rapidly declines after this and they often accumulate viruses.

Pruning

Rambling roses do not need to be pruned in order to grow healthily, and by and large are best left to their own devices to sprawl up a large tree or over a building, but if they are too big or are being trained in any way, then they should be pruned as soon as they have finished flowering, which will by and large be by the beginning of August. Remove any old or unwanted stems right to the ground and cut the remainder back to an open two-dimensional framework, remembering that flowers will be produced on the growth made over the remainder of the summer.

Hedges

Young birds will have left their nests, so August is a good month to cut all hedges. Start by cutting the sides. Be sure to make a 'batter' – that is, to ensure that the base of the hedge is wider than the top – regardless of the height. This allows light to reach the bottom half and ensures full, healthy foliage down to the ground. Then cut the top, using string as a guide to keep it straight and level. If it is an informal hedge, curve the top over so it is rounded.

All unprickly summer hedge trimmings, including yew and box, which are soft and include lots of foliage, can be mown, gathered into the grass collector and put on the compost heap.

September

The September garden thins out, as though the colours and light were being gently stretched. The sun drops in the sky, slanting at an angle that, for a few precious weeks, creates the best light of the year, and the thinning leaves sieve it like muslin. Above all, there is a real sense that the year is slipping away. The days are often hot enough for shirtsleeves and a sprawl on the dry grass, and the evenings cool enough for a jersey and a fire to light the failing days. All the edges are softened but not blunted.

But, despite this, it is also the month of blazing colour. All the plants that originate from close to the equator continue to fill the borders with splashes of bright, strong colour (especially if you can keep up the increasingly demanding job of deadheading).

September is a time of refinement and generosity, of largesse dispensed in the knowledge that the days of wine and roses are coming to an end so should be savoured all the more.

All the plants that originate from close to the equator continue to fill the borders with splashes of bright, strong colour

Our dahlias love our heavy soil and seem to get better and better throughout the month. As long as there is no frost, then they relish the conditions and are not at all bothered by the shortening days. This I think is what I love most about September – that unique mixture between hot, bright days blazing with exotic colour, and the gently falling light that adds subtlety to these final days of summer.

The secret of keeping the September flower garden vibrant is to deadhead daily, taking off every fading flower to provoke the equatorial plants such as tithonias, cosmos, zinnias and dahlias, to produce more buds for as long as the days (or more critically, the nights) stay warm enough. As with all deadheading, do not just pull off the spent petals but cut back to a leaf or side shoot.

....

Semi-ripe cuttings

September is the ideal month for semi-ripe cuttings. These can be taken from woody herbs like rosemary, lavender or thyme, from soft fruit such as gooseberries and redcurrants, as well as from any flowering shrubs such as roses.

Whereas softwood cuttings are taken entirely from new growth (and are usually taken earlier in the year), semi-ripe cuttings are taken from current season's wood that has started to harden off a little. The tip is soft and bendy but the base of the cutting will have wood that has started to become more rigid.

A plant grown from a cutting will always be exactly the same as its parent plant, whereas one grown from seed will always be different. Cuttings are essentially clones, so if you have a favourite rose or a particularly delicious gooseberry or a really good upright rosemary bush, then all these qualities will remain with the new plants grown from cuttings.

Before you set out to take any cuttings, have with you a plastic bag and a sharp knife or secateurs. The bag is for placing the cut material immediately into to reduce moisture loss, and the sharper your cutting implements, the more likely your cuttings are to root.

Always choose healthy, strong, straight growth, free from any flowers or flower buds, for cutting material. Once you have taken material from the plant and placed it in the polythene bag, it's important to act quickly. The cuttings are effectively dying from the second you cut them until they develop new roots, so the quicker you can work, the more likely you are to have success.

Strip off all lower leaves and side shoots so that only an inch or less of foliage remains. Leaving too much increases the loss of moisture via

transpiration. Cut the bare stem to size with a sharp knife or secateurs, and bury it in a container of very gritty or sandy compost.

It is best to place the cuttings around the edge of a pot. You can always get at least four and often more in one container. Put this somewhere warm and bright but not on a south-facing windowsill as this may scorch them. Water well and then a daily spray with a mister will help stop the leaves drying out before new roots have time to form. You will know that the roots have formed when you see fresh new growth. At that point, the cuttings can be potted on individually to grow on.

Since box blight arrived in the garden a few years ago, I have been taking a lot of yew cuttings before trimming the yew hedges and topiary to keep them sharp all winter, thus creating hundreds of healthy yew plants for free.

I take cuttings from plants with vigorous growth, and either cut a good straight shoot about 6in long or peel a bushy side shoot, retaining a slight 'heel' or section of the stem that it was attached to. The former will always be more upright and perhaps faster-growing, and the latter more bushy, so from the outset you can determine the best cuttings for different uses.

They will start to show signs of growth next spring and can be potted on or lined out as individual plants next autumn, to grow into useable bushes in two or three years' time.

Now is a good time to trim any evergreen hedging or topiary to keep them crisp throughout winter – and this will also provide you with the material for your cuttings.

September is also the ideal month for planting evergreens so the roots can get established before winter.

Spring bulbs

Bulbs of spring-flowering plants such as daffodils, crocuses, muscari, wood anemones and scillas, can all be planted as soon as the ground is soft enough in September (although it is often bone dry and impossible to dig into turf, especially under trees, until next month). These bulbs all start to grow long before the first shoots appear in the new year, so the sooner they get into the ground, the better the root system and potential flowering they will have. Except for snowdrops and fritillaries, good drainage is the key to successful bulbs, and by and large, the deeper you can plant the bulbs, the better.

Every September I plant a batch of fresh bulbs into pots filled with a particularly free-draining compost

I love the early irises such as *Iris reticulata* or *I. histrioides*, but they do not do well in our wet soil, so every September I plant a batch of fresh bulbs into pots filled with a particularly free-draining compost. These then can be set aside in a cool but not too wet corner until the buds appear, when they can be moved to a position where the exquisite flowers can be best enjoyed.

Fruit and veg

September's harvest is dominated by all the vegetables that we borrow briefly from much warmer parts of the world – melons, peppers, tomatoes, pumpkins, fennel and beans, as well as those like apples, plums and pears, and the hardy vegetables that are still growing well.

The old brown canes of summer-fruiting raspberries can all be cut down to the ground, leaving the fresh new green canes standing. These will carry next summer's crop. Reduce the new canes to a maximum of six strong growths per plant. These remaining canes will need holding securely for the next year, therefore summer raspberries are best grown against a permanent system of support. I tie the canes with twine to parallel wires fixed strongly between robust posts, fanning them out evenly as I work along the wire at each level. It is important that they are really secure as winter winds can catch and damage the canes.

I check the apples and pears daily, weighing and turning any in my hands that seem ripe, hoping that they will gently come away at that perfect moment of ripeness. There is nothing that you can do now to improve the quality or quantity of the harvest, but care will infinitely improve the way that apples, in particular, store. Any that are cracked or bruised will not keep but if you have a garage or shed, you can keep undamaged apples well into the new year.

Dahlias

Dahlias will keep producing new flowers well into autumn as long as they are deadheaded regularly from late summer. The easiest way to tell the difference between a spent flower and an emerging bud is by the shape: buds are invariably rounded whereas a spent flower is pointed and cone-shaped. Always cut back to the next side shoot – even if it means taking a long stem – as this will stimulate new flowers and avoid ugly spikes of stem.

October

Almost no other month has the capacity for change like October. It can come in as late summer and four weeks later leave you in the grip of winter. But one of the side effects of climate change is that our gardens are flowering longer with better autumnal displays.

But there is a real sense of all this being left over from a previous season. Every sunny day is borrowed and the light – although often the most golden of the whole year – is slipping away. There comes a moment in October when you realise that the garden is weary of all that busy growing and flowering, and the setting of seeds and fruits. You can sense it is running out of steam.

And, if I am honest, this gardener, too, feels the batteries run low. The dark evenings that are so frustrating in spring or even September come as a relief in October and are a welcome excuse to go indoors and shut the garden outside in the growing dark.

I clear the tomatoes from the greenhouse in early October

I clear the tomatoes from the greenhouse in early October because it gives me space to plant out the young salad seedlings that I sowed in August. I choose varieties of lettuce such as 'Merveille de Quatre Saisons' and 'Bruin d'Hiver' as well as hardy crops such as rocket, mizuna and mibuna, which will all benefit from the protection of the glass but not need any extra heat through the winter. If these are put into the tomato beds – which will be dug over and refreshed with a dressing of garden compost – they quickly get established in the warm soil and this provides us with plants big enough to provide a daily salad to eat once the outdoor plants are over some time in November.

They then sit quietly, small but delicious, until February when they

start to grow again as the days get longer.

I regard October's fallen leaves as a precious harvest and every leaf is carefully raked and kept to make leafmould, which we use as an important element in our potting compost and as a mulch for woodland plants. If the leaves are not too wet, we try and mow as many as possible – often placing them on a brick path to do so – because they decompose very much faster if chopped up and then kept damp. Because leafmould is made largely by fungal rather than bacterial activity, there is no need to turn it but we simply store the gathered leaves in a wire-sided bay or in bin bags and by next October they will be a lovely, rich compost.

Bringing tender plants indoors

There is always a time in October when a call has to be made and tender plants such as citrus in pots or bananas, cannas, salvias and dahlias growing in borders, have to be brought into the greenhouse before they are damaged. But the more cold that they are exposed to, the hardier they become and therefore the less vulnerable to cold weather, so I try and delay that moment as long as possible without damaging them.

Autumn raspberries will fruit from late July through to December in a mild autumn and are always prolific throughout October. They demand almost no attention other than supporting from midsummer to stop them flopping all over the place and to make it easier to pick the fruit, and cutting back and removing all growth in the new year, followed by as thick a mulch as you can provide. This can be almost anything weed-suppressing – I used old hay this year – but never use mushroom compost as it is too alkaline. They need no protection from the blackbirds, who can be rapacious of the summer-fruiting varieties but seem to have had their raspberry fill by the time that the autumn-fruiting varieties bear their harvest. I grow 'Autumn Bliss' and the yellow 'Golden Everest'. Both are very prolific and delicious.

Hardwood cuttings

Softwood cuttings – usually taken from new shoots and formed of entirely pliable growth – root very quickly but also die very quickly so the window of rooting opportunity is very brief. Semi-ripe cuttings are slower to root but have a greater chance of surviving and need less mollycoddling, but hardwood cuttings are the easiest of the lot, needing no protection at all although producing their new roots very slowly.

For hardwood cuttings you use wood that has ripened after a full summer's growth – the best way to judge this is that none of it should be bendy – and any time between October and Christmas is a good time to take them. An ideal candidate is any favourite rose or indeed any shrub that has good straight growth formed over the past few months.

1. **Choose** healthy straight stems of new growth without any flower buds on them and with at least 12in of growth about the thickness of a pencil.
2. **Divide** the stems into lengths about 9in long, cutting horizontally across the bottom section and diagonally across the top so you remember which way up to insert the cuttings.
3. **Mix** plenty of grit into the soil to lighten it, then make a slit trench by inserting the full depth of the spade and levering the soil apart. Then insert each cutting about 3in apart and with only an inch showing above ground. Backfill and water. Leave the cuttings for 12 months before transplanting or potting up.

Sweet peas

Sweet peas flower earlier, more frequently and for longer if they have a strong root system. The best way to ensure that is to sow them as early as possible so that when you plant them out in April, they are strong, sturdy plants with robust roots. Obviously this cannot be done outside because it is too cold for them to germinate and grow, but if you sow them now, within the protection of a greenhouse, cold frame or porch, this gives them a chance to get a head start.

Sweet peas have a long taproot so whatever you sow them in must have room for this to grow. You can sow them in a deep seed tray but they will need pricking out as soon as possible. Much better to sow two or three seeds to a 3in pot or one seed per root trainer or large plug, and let them remain in this container undisturbed until planting. They do not need any extra heat to germinate as long as the temperature is around 10–15°C. The seedlings need no protection other than to be kept frost-free.

Other jobs for the month

1. **Climate** change is delaying the onset of cold weather in autumn but there is no guarantee that there will not be a hard frost in October. If you do not already possess them, invest in horticultural fleece and some cloches – and be sure to use them before you need them. Cloches are very good for rows of vegetables, keeping them dry as well as warm (although I always leave the ends open – I'm happy to trade some heat for some ventilation) and fleece is the best temporary protection against frost, either laid out over small plants or draped over shrubs and bushes.

2. **Sow** a row or two of 'Aquadulce' broad beans if the soil is dry enough.

3. **Garlic** can be planted any time in October although hard-necked varieties should be planted first as they take longer to grow. Prepare the ground so that it is raked to a fine tilth and plant the cloves in rows about 6–9in apart and with the top of the pointed end an inch below the surface. In a good year, I keep the biggest and best of my own bulbs for seed for the following year but always buy in fresh stock after that. Use healthy fat bulbs for seed, and only plant the outer cloves. Keep the inner ones, which are smaller, for cooking. The bigger the clove, the better the chance of a big bulb growing from it.

4. **Keep** deadheading throughout October, particularly the short-day plants like dahlias. This will extend their flowering season and squeeze the last bloom from them.

5. **Save** yourself a fortune by collecting seeds from perennial plants, using paper (not polythene) bags. Always label seed packets

immediately because you will forget what they contain! Store in a cool, dry place until ready for sowing.

6. **It** is worth taking trouble to store the fruit so that it lasts as long as possible. I am often tempted to store apples that have only slight bruising or damage. It is a mistake. Only store perfect apples, which discounts all windfalls. As well as being vulnerable to frost and rodents, apples dry out as they store, so they need to be kept somewhere cool and humid. A cellar is ideal, or a garage or shed, but polythene bags, folded not tied, and punctured with pencil holes, work very well. Put the bags somewhere cool and dark.

7. **You** can plant or move deciduous trees shrubs and hedges even if they are still in leaf, as they have finished growing and the soil is still warm so the roots will begin to grow immediately. It is essential, of course, to give them a good soak when you plant them and to repeat this weekly until the ground is really wet or the leaves have fallen.

8. **Plant** or move biennials such as forget-me-nots, wallflowers, foxgloves, onorpordums and mulleins to their intended flowering position for next spring and summer.

9. **Continue** planting spring bulbs but wait another month before beginning to plant tulips.

10. **Keep** cutting the grass for as long as it keeps growing, however it is better to have the grass too long than too short over the winter months. Rake out thatch and moss and add to the compost heap.

11. **October** is the perfect time to aerate your lawn. Reducing compaction will do more to ensure healthy grass next year than anything else. For small areas, this can be done by working a fork as deeply as possible all over the surface of the lawn. For larger lawns it is worth hiring a dedicated aerator to do the job.

12. **Cut** off any hellebore leaves that are obviously diseased and mulch around spring-flowering perennials with a 50:50 mix of last year's leafmould and garden compost.

13. **Prune** climbing roses by removing old stems and any damaged or crossing new growth, and by cutting all lateral shoots back to a healthy leaf bud.

14. **Tie** all climbers up securely to protect them from winter wind damage.
15. **Give** deciduous hedges a light trim in October, which will keep them crisp through the winter and looking good when everything else has sunk into decline.

November

The November days draw in like a noose and the garden seems to slowly implode, losing all the things that gave it worth. The only answer to this is to tend it like an ailing friend, both to honour its better days and to prepare for the inevitable recovery in the New Year.

And there can be wonderful days, particularly at the beginning of the month, when the leaves are still holding on and glowing golden in the thin but clear light. This, rather than October, is the month when the leaves reach their best autumnal colour, as well as when they really start to stream from the trees in earnest, although wet weather followed by a sharp frost – which November invariably brings – will send them not drifting in the breeze, but clattering down in the still air and hitting the ground like smashing crockery.

It is a good idea to leave as much winter cover as possible, which provides insulation and a microclimate to protect plants from the coldest weather, seedheads for birds, and is important cover for insects. Plants with dry, hollow stems such as asters, heleniums, rudbeckias and all grasses are especially good and should be left untouched until spring.

But at least half of all summer's growth can be removed, especially if it is wet and soggy and falling over the crowns of plants, as this can cause them to rot. Start by cutting back anything that is not standing well without support. It is important not to snip timidly but to make any cuts right at the base of the plants, removing the whole of the intended stem or leaf. This will let air in and help clear up and prevent fungal problems.

It is a mistake to provide more than minimal heat to citrus plants during the winter months, with a range of 5–15°C being ideal. Although they should be watered very sparingly – once a month is adequate – the air should be damp and cool, so in general, a conservatory or indoor room will be too dry, whereas a frost-free greenhouse or even a

shed works very well.

Any salad crops that have been growing through early autumn are liable to be nipped by the first frosts and will almost stop growing completely as the days get shorter and the light levels lower. However simply by cloching them I have found that their season can be extended almost into spring. I do not close the ends of the cloches but allow the air to go through for ventilation. This is especially important for chicory, which is very hardy but hates the mixture of cold and wet, and will easily rot, forming a slimy, brown carapace over otherwise untouched leaves.

Dahlias and cannas

Dahlias will continue flowering until the first frosts. The top growth can be completely blackened by frost without the tubers being damaged. But the combination of wet and frozen ground is too much for them, so unless you have very good drainage or the winter temperatures rarely drop below −5°C, then it is best to lift the tubers and store them. Before putting them away for the winter months, the top growth should be cut back, leaving just 6in of stem. At this point label them very clearly! Dahlias should have any damp soil removed and be left to dry upside down for a day or two for the hollow stems to drain. They should then be packed in crates or pots with sand, spent potting compost or even sawdust. This will insulate them and absorb excess moisture without their drying out completely.

Cannas are also too tender to leave out all winter and are best potted into leafmould or used potting compost, then watered and placed somewhere cool. Beneath a bench in a frost-free greenhouse works well. Water them lightly every few weeks so that they do not actively grow but never dry out.

December

In December the garden is stripped of all dignity as well as of colour and foliage. The star that strode the summer stage is huddling on the street. And the greatest humiliation is not the grey or rain or drifts of sodden leaves and rotting stems, but the brown.

There is only one adequate solution and that is to add as much green as possible to your winter. Green saves the day, the month, the year. Green endures and sustains in a way that no other colour can begin to match. Evergreen hedges do not just add structural 'bones' to a garden but, above all, a matrix of green that defies the depths of midwinter in a way that no flowers ever could. They are the essential evergreen structure holding the garden together until spring returns.

December is when I batten down the hatches and try to sort things out behind the scenes. The truth is that I rarely do much of that. It is the worst month of the year for any gardener.

Green saves the day, the month, the year. Green endures and sustains in a way that no other colour can begin to match

I do less gardening in the whole month of December than I do in a normal week of March or April. In fact, there have been some Decembers when I have barely done anything at all other than open up the greenhouses occasionally. The combination of the shortest days and the wettest, dreariest weather means that the garden shuts up shop and hunkers down, waiting for the year to pass. But occasionally there are a few days of dry weather and I try and get out and clear as much fallen, soggy foliage from the borders as possible. Anything standing without support is left as cover for the birds and to add a skeletal adornment to the garden, but a soggy carapace of rotting vegetation never does any good.

Although I am sure there are conscientious gardeners who wash and oil every tool after use and keep all their cutting tools from hoe to scythe honed to a state of permanent razor-sharpness, for most of us these things inevitably slip amidst the busyness of summer gardening.

But come December and there is no excuse. If it is hammering with rain outside or simply so cold your fingers cannot function, you can still go through all your tools and make sure that they are in as good condition as possible for next year.

One of the most satisfying jobs is to clean and sharpen all cutting implements. Hoes can be sharpened with a rough whetstone so they slice through weeds rather than bruise them, and secateurs can have all rust removed with wire wool and a little elbow grease, and then be sharpened as you would a knife so that they can cut easily and accurately. Sharp secateurs are both better for the plant because they leave a neat, clean cut rather than tearing at it, and much safer for the gardener because you can focus on where and how you are cutting rather than trying to force it at all.

Finally, the rhythm of the year does not follow the calendar but the light. So, in the week between Christmas and New Year, I tentatively reintroduce myself to the garden. The days have no further to fall and the only way is up. The weather is likely to be bad and the pleasures very brief. But it is a beginning.

Index

Page numbers in *italics* indicate
illustrations. Page numbers in
bold refer to a main section or
entry.

A

acanthus 73–4
agapanthus 79
  May 226
  modern urban gardens 81
alliums:
  cottage gardens 71
  May 225
  summer 12
  see also garlic; onions
Alpine strawberries 198
annuals 114
  containers 98
  cottage gardens 69, 71, 72
  growing 152
  herbs 180–1
  July 235–6
  June 229, 232
  March 216
  May 226
  small town gardens 56
  winter 19, 22
ants 120
aphids 96, **134**
  apple trees 160
  feed 101, 102, 153
  insecticides 85
  winter 18
apples 14
  blossom 225
  cottage gardens 66
  pruning 159–60, 239
  September 249–50
  spurs 205

storage 256
types 186–7
apricots 189–90, 205
April 11, **220–4**
aquilegias:
  cottage gardens 66, 68
  May 225
architectural plants 81–3
artichokes 232–3, 235
asparagus 228
asters 69
August 12, **240–4**
autumn 14–18
  raspberries 198, 253
  see also November; October;
    September

B

bacteria 27, 142
bamboos 82
banana plants *76*, 77
  May 226
  modern urban gardens 81
bare-root plants 208–9
basil 181
bay 18, 180
beans 174, 230
  August 241
  July 235, 237
  sowing 255
  see also broad beans
bees 10, *29*
  attracting 28
  plants for 86
  wildlife gardening 94–5
beetles 88
beetroot 174
  August 241
  July 235

berries *193*, 196–9
  August 242
biennials:
  cottage gardens 69, 71, 72
  July 235–6
  October 256
  spring 19
  winter 22
birch 15, 17
birds 92–3
  April 220–1
  fruit 192, 196, 197
  winter 22–3
black spot 129
blackberries 199
blackbirds 92, 192
  strawberries 197
blackcurrants 196
blight 128, 178, 238, 241
bluebells 225
borders:
  containers 106
  cottage gardens 65, 66
  July 235, 237
  June 230
  March 218
  size 34, 51
  small town gardens 56
  structure 33
  summer 12
brassicas 178
  succession sowing 174, 176
broad beans 210, 255
buddleia:
  August 240
  colour 42
  cottage gardens 68
  pruning 162, 213
bulbs 11

cottage gardens 71
  January 206
  modern urban gardens 82
  planting 256
  September 248–9
  wildlife gardening 92
  winter 22
buttercups 122
butterflies 86, 88
  brassicas 132, 134

C

cacti 81
camellias 112
  modern urban gardens 81
  shade 103
  winter 18
canker 129
cannas 77–8
  exotic gardens 74
  July 235
  June 232
  May 226
  October 253
  winter potting 260
cardoons 69, 73, 79
carrots 174, 176
  July 235
caterpillars 132, *133*, 134
catkins 10, 208
ceanothus 81
  pruning 162, 213
  south-facing 111
celery 174
chafer grubs 120
chard 174, 177–8
  August 241
chemicals 85
  pests 130
  strawberries 197
  weeds 124
  wildlife gardening 94, 96
chicken-wire:
  leafmould *16*, 18
  rabbits 131
chicory 174

August 241
June 230
children 54, 97
chillies 206
chitting 209–10
chives 183
citrus plants 226, 258, 260
clematis 59, *109*, *110*
  August 240
  cottage gardens 68, 69
  fungi 129
  pruning 158, 162, 213
  summer 12
  supporting 113
climate change 154, 251, 255
climbers **108–13**
  containers 106
  cottage gardens 69
  exotic gardens 78–9
  pruning 211
  small town gardens 59
  supporting 112–13, 217
  tying up 257
  winter 22
cloches 255, 260
cold frames 153, 173
  hardening off 224
  herbs 181
  March 216–17
  slug protection 132
  sweet peas 254
colour **42–7**
  cottage gardens 66, *67*, 68, 71
  emotional effect 45, 47
  leaves 15, 258
  light 44–5
  September 245
  summer 12
  theme 42
  tulips 221
  west-facing 112
compass points 108, 111–12
compost **140–2**
  containers 100–1, *143*
  definition 140–1
  fungi 129

January 206
  making 141–2
  moisture 142
  shrubs 114
  vegetables 206
  wildlife gardening 96
  see also leafmould; mulch
containers **98–107**
  at a glance 107
  compost 100–1
  cuttings 248
  design 98, 100, 105–7
  drainage 101
  exotic gardens 74
  figs 190
  problems 102–3
  seasonal 11, 52
  shade 103, 105
  small town gardens 57–8
  tomatoes 238
  vegetables 172
  water features 61
  watering 101–2
cordons 191, 205
  pruning 160, 162
  tomatoes 238
coriander 180, 181
cornus: pruning 162, 213
cosmos 71, *201*
  August 240
  July 235
  June 232
  May 226
  September 246
  summer 12
Cottage Garden 45
cottage gardens **65–72**
  at a glance 72
  borders 51
  colour 45, 47, *67*
  plants 68–71
cow parsley *70*, 225
crocuses 92
  February 208
  March 215
  planting 248

crop rotation 176
currants *194*, 195–6
cuttings 254
  pelargonium 224
  semi-ripe 246, 248

D
daffodils:
  cottage gardens 71
  March 215
  planting 248
  spring 10, 11
  wildlife gardening 92
dahlias 12
  August 240
  containers 74
  cottage gardens 71
  earwigs 138–9
  exotic gardens 74
  July 235
  June 232
  March 216
  May 226
  November 260
  October 253, 255
  September 245, 246, 250
  tree dahlia 78
dandelions 94, 122
day length:
  August 240
  autumn 14
  March 215
  May 226
  October 251
  spring 10, 11
deadheading 162, 245–6
  dahlias 250
  October 255
  roses 237
December **261–2**
deciduous trees 19, 159
delphiniums 66, 68, 69
design **32–9**
  containers 105–7
  cottage gardens 65–6
  divisions and dimensions

34, 36, 51–2, 58–9
  see also colour
drainage:
  containers 98, 100, 101–2
  dry conditions 79
  herbs 180
  vegetables 171
dry conditions 79, 171
dry shade 74, 105

E
earwigs 138–9
east-facing walls 112
easterly winds 24
elm 15
espaliers 191, 205, 239
  pruning 160, 162
evergreens:
  birds 84
  modern urban gardens 81
  planting 148, 248
  pruning 162
  wind 19–20
exotic gardens **73–80**
  at a glance 80
experts, gardening 8–9, 157

F
'fairy rings' 120, 128
fan training 191, 205
  pruning 160, 162
February 11, **208–14**
feeding:
  containers 100–1, 107
fences 52
  climbers 59
  rabbits 131
fennel 66, 184, 241
ferns:
  containers 105
  exotic gardens 74
  modern urban gardens 81
  moisture 60, 62, 105
  shade *55*
  types 61–2
figs 190

fleece 14, 22, 255
  banana plants 77
  ferns 74
  fruit 189
  perennials 226
  tree dahlia 78
  vegetables 171
flowers 11, 12, 51
  deadheading 245–6
  shrubs 116, 213
  wild 91–2
  wildlife 86
  see also individual flowers
foliage 12
  exotic gardens 73
  wind 25
  see also leaf fall
food **166–71**; *see also* fruit;
  herbs; vegetables
food chain 84–5, 93
forget-me-nots 71, 256
foxgloves 256
  cottage gardens 66, 71
frogs 88, 91
frost 20, 22
  exotic gardens 80
  protection 255, 260
fruit:
  fungi 129
  pruning 160, 162
  soft **192–9**, 205–6, 242
  supporting 112
  top **186–91**, 204–5, 239,
    249–50
  see also individual fruits
fuchsia 213, 226
fungi 27, **128–9**
  lawns 120
  problems 128
  role of 27
  types 129

G
garden styles:
  cottage 65–72
  exotic 73–80

modern urban 81–3
small town 54–64
wildlife 84–96
garlic 178, 237
August 241
July 235, 237
October 255
planting 255
succession sowing 174
gooseberries 196, 205–6
cuttings 246
pruning 162
grass 27, 34
cutting 92, 213–14
length 85, 95
October 256
wildlife 85, 91–2
see also lawns
greenhouse:
annuals 71
citrus plants 258
dahlias 260
hardening off 224
herbs 181, 184
October 251, 253
onions 210
salad crops 210
seedlings 173
slug protection 132
sweet peas 254
tomatoes 177, 237
tulips 206
woodlice 135
growing **152–7**
see also fruit; herbs; vegetables

H
hard surfaces:
colour 47
cottage gardens 72
small town gardens 57
see also walls
hardening off 224, 226
hardwood cuttings 254
hedges:
cutting *164*, 165, 244

design 33, 36
hawthorn 215
height 36
small town gardens 58
structure 33
topiary 163
trimming 234, 248, 257
wildlife 84, 85–6
heleniums 42, 240
helianthus 12, 69
hellebores 11
cottage gardens 68
February 208
March 215
herbaceous plants 22
herbs **180–5**
compost 100
cottage gardens 66
hoeing 124–5, 226
honeysuckle 112
cottage gardens 69
pruning 158
supporting 113
horseradish 185
hostas 54, 73
April 223
ponds 91
shade *55*, 56
slugs 85, 102
humus 140–1
hydrangeas 111, 159

I
insecticides 85
insects 26, 93
earwigs 138–9
lawns 120
wasps 137–8
see also bees
irises 11
containers 249
cottage gardens 68
May 225
modern urban gardens 82–3
ponds 91
irrigation 80

containers 101–2
exotic gardens 80
ivy *59*, 111

J
January 11, **204–6**
jasmine 18, 59
exotic gardens 79
Jewel Garden 12, *13*, *43*
clematis *109*
colour 43, 44–5, 47
containers *104*, 105
July 12, **235–9**
June 12, **229–34**

K L
kale 178
lavender:
compost 100
containers 107
cottage gardens 66, 68
cuttings 246
May 226
modern urban gardens 81
pruning 159
lawns 51, 56–7, **117–20**
aeration 256
children 97
fungi 128–9
leaf fall 15, 17, 253
leafmould *16*, 17–18, 253
leaves 15, 17, 27; *see also*
foliage
lettuce *175*, 177
aphids 134
February 210
October 251
planting 251
slugs 131–2
sowing 241
light 14, 15, 33
colour 44
February 210
lilac 68, 233–4
lilies 71
lovage 183

lupins 12
  cottage gardens 66, 68, 69

M
mahonia 56, 81
maple 60
March 11, **215–18**
  planting 148
marigolds 42, 69, 91
marjoram 184
May 11, 12, **225–8**
measuring 48
  ponds 89
  raised beds 177
Mediterranean herbs 180
melianthus 18, 79
microclimates 19, 25
mint 66, 183
modern urban gardens **81–3**
moisture:
  compost 142
  cuttings 246, 248
  dahlias 260
  exotic gardens 79, 80
  ferns 60, 62, 105
  figs 190
  lawns 118
  mulch 125–6, 217
  raspberries 198
  soil 174
  strawberries 197
  tomatoes 238
  vegetables 169
  weeds 226
moles 28, 130–1
morello cherries 112, 191
morning glory 59, 79, 106
mulch 217–18
  cannas 78
  moisture 125–6, 217
  shrubs 114
  weeds 125–6

N
names 200
nature **26–8**; *see also* wildlife

  gardening
nectarines 189
nestboxes 93
netting:
  berries 197
  currants 196
  pigeons 135
  wind 19
new garden plot **48–53**
  at a glance 53
  design 49, 51
  divisions 51–2
  local environment 49
north-facing walls 111
northerly winds 24
November 78, **258–60**

O
October 148, **251–7**
onions 210, 241
orchards *see* apples

P
palms 74, 77
parsley 181, 241
paths:
  cottage gardens 65–6
  design 33–4
  types 40
peaches 189, 205
pears 187, 249–50
  pruning 162, 239
  spurs 205
peas 174, 235, 237
pelargoniums 224
  compost 100
  containers 107
  May 226
peonies 68, 69
peppers 230, 241
perennials:
  April 220
  containers 98
  cottage gardens 68–9, 72
  herbs 183–4
  March 216

mulch 217–18, 256
  seeds 255–6
  small town gardens 55
  staking 237
  supporting 237
  winter 20, 22
pests 28, **130–9**
  caterpillars 132, 134
  earwigs 138–9
  moles 130–1
  pigeons 135
  rabbits 131
  rats 136
  squirrels 136–7
  voles 136
  wasps 137–8
  woodlice 135
  see also aphids; slugs; vine
    weevils
philadelphus 68, 213
phlox 66, 69
pigeons 135
place 30–1, 37
  plants 154, 157
planning **48–53**
  autumn 14–15
  cottage gardens 65–8
  divisions 51–2
  height 52
  local environment 49
  modern urban gardens 81–2
  new plot 48–9
  small town gardens 54, 56–7
  soil 53
  see also design
planting **148–50**
  climbers 59, 112
  containers 107
  cottage gardens 66
  holes 114, 148–50, 216
  March 216
  May 226, 228
  October 256
  ponds 91
  shrubs 114
  strawberries 197

plants:
  bare-root 208–9
  biennials 69, 71
  containers 103, 105
  design 37, 39
  exotic gardens 73–4, 79, 80
  ferns 61–2
  growing 153–4, 157
  hardening off 224, 226
  modern urban gardens 81–2
  palms 74, 77
  placement 154, 157
  ponds 91
  pruning 158–60
  shade-loving 55, 56
  species 152–3
  supporting 237
  tender 232, 253
  wind 25
  winter 18–20, 22
  see also annuals; bulbs;
    climbers; colour; flowers;
    herbs; perennials; shrubs
plums 187, 205
pollinators 10, 94, 186
ponds 86–91
  August 241–2
  clearing *87*, 242
  making 89, 91
  marginal planting 88, *90*, 91
  modern urban gardens 82–3
poppies 68, 225
potatoes 178, 235, 237
  chitting 209–10
pots *see* containers
potting compost 100–1, 206
primroses 10, 11
  containers 107
  cottage gardens 68
  February 208
  March 215
private space 34, 59
pruning **158–65**
  August 244
  blackcurrants 196
  February 211, 213

fruit trees 186, 187, 190,
  204–5, 239
hedges *164*, 165
June 233–4
March 216
modern urban gardens 82
October 256
redcurrants 195–6
shrubs 114
summer 162
timing 158–9
topiary 163
winter 160, 162

Q R

quinces 112, *188*, 189
rabbits 131
radishes 12
raised beds *170*, 176–7
  compost 210
raspberries 198–9
  autumn 253
  January 205–6
  pruning 249
rats 136
redcurrants *194*, 195–6
  cuttings 246
  January 205–6
  pruning 162
rhubarb 66
  growing 192, 195, 215–16
rills 83
rocket 168, 173, 177
  April 223
  August 240, 241
  cottage gardens 71
  February 210
  October 251, 253
  spring 12
  succession sowing 174
  winter 22
rosemary 66, 81, 180
  cuttings 246
roses:
  autumn 14
  black spot 129

cottage gardens 66, 69
cuttings 246
deadheading 237
pruning 162, 211, 213, 244,
  256
south-facing 111
species 225, 230, 232
summer 12
west-facing *62*, 112

S

salad *see* lettuce; rocket; tomatoes
salvias 18
  August 240
  July 235
  June 232
  May 226
sawflies 195, 196
scab 129
scale plans 48–9
scent 79, 116
seasons **10–23**
  autumn 14–18
  containers 98, 107
  fruit 192, 198
  growing 154
  hedges 164, 165
  planting 148
  pruning 160, 162
  small town gardens 56
  spring 10–12
  summer 12
  vegetables 174
  winter 18–23
  see also individual months
seating 34, **40–1**
  small town gardens 54, 57
seedlings 168–9
  herbs 181, 183
  planting *151*
  vegetables 173
seeds 255–6
semi-ripe cuttings 246, 248
September 12, **245–50**
  strawberries 197
shade *55*, 56

containers 103, 105
ferns 61–2, 74
shrubs 116
small town gardens 56
times of day 103
shrubs **114–16**
cottage gardens 68
March 216
planting 148–9
pruning 158–9, 162, 213
seasons 52
wildlife 86
winter 22
slugs 18, 85, 131–2
vegetables 178
small town gardens **54–64**
at a glance 62, 64
climbers 59
shrubs 116
trees 60
water features 60–1
snails 18
vegetables 178
snowdrops:
containers 107
cottage gardens 71
February 208
spring 10, 11
wildlife gardening 92
soft fruit **192–9**
August 242
pruning 160, 162
September 249
soil:
frozen 19, 20
herbs 180
humus 140–1
moisture 79, 174
pH 49
preparation 53, 56, 80
raised beds *170*, 176–7
shrubs 116
spring 10–11
types 49, 116, 121
vegetables 174, 176
warmth 10, 173

weeds 121–2, 125
winter 18
worms 27–8
sorrel 184
south-facing walls 108, 111
southerly winds 24
sowing 10–11
August 241
March 216–17
succession 169, 174
vegetables 173–4
space 36
containers 106–7
private 34
small town gardens 58–9, 64
spiraea 162, 213
spring 10–12; *see also* April;
March; May
Spring Garden *70*
squirrels 136–7
staking 149, 237
strawberries *193*, 196–8
Alpine 198
August 242
streams 60–1
succession sowing 12, 169, 174
summer 12
colour 44
herbs 181, 183
pruning 162
raspberries 198–9
see also August; July; June
sun:
autumn 14
colours 44
containers 102, 103
design 36
evening 240
ferns 74
figs 190
frost 20
fruit 186, 187, 197
herbs 184
lawns 118
ponds 88
seating 34, 40–1

vegetables 173, 177, 233
sunflowers 12
August 240
cottage gardens 69
July 235
supports 112–13
borders 237
March 217
raspberries 198–9, 249
see also wigwams
swallows 23, 220–1
sweet peas 112–13
August 240
containers 106
cottage gardens 69
July 235
October 254–5
wigwams 59, 66
sweetcorn 230, 241

T

tarragon 180, 184, 226
tayberries 199
temperature:
summer 12
vegetables 169, 171
winter 19, 20
thyme 59, 180, *182*
cuttings 246
tithonias:
August 240
colour 42
June 232
September 246
summer 12
tomatoes 177, **238–9**
August 241
June 230
leaf removal 241
moisture 239
temperature 12
tools **144–6**, *147*, 262
top fruit **186–91**
pruning 160, 239
September 249–50
topiary 163, 248

modern urban gardens 82
training 191, 205, 239
trees 33
  autumn 15, 17
  birds 92–3
  March 216
  planting 38, 148–9
  pruning 158–60
  roots 149
  small garden 59, 60
  wildlife 86
  winter 22
  see also fruit: top; leaf
    fall
trellising 52, 59, 113
tulips 71
  containers *104*, 105
  April 221, 222
  January 206
  wildlife gardening 92

U V

umbellifers 134
untidiness 27–8, 95
vegetables 169, 171, **172–9**
  April 223
  artichokes 232–3
  asparagus 228
  at a glance 179
  August 240–1
  caterpillars 132, *133*, 134
  compost 206
  cottage gardens 66
  essential 177–8
  February 209–10
  July 237–9
  June 230
  moisture 169
  September 249
  soil 174, 176

sowing 173–4
spring 11–12
weeds 124–5
see also individual vegetables
vine weevils 103, 134–5
voles 136

W

Walled Garden *50*, *63*
wallflowers 69, 71, 256
walls 108, 111–12
  climbers 59
wasps 137–8
water features 33, **60–1**
  modern urban gardens 82–3
  ponds 86–91, 241–2
  wildlife gardening 95
watering 171
  containers 101–2
  shrubs 114
weather **24–5**
  autumn 15
  birds 221
  March 215
  May 225
  sowing 173
  winter 18
  see also frost; wind
weeds **121–7**, 226
  dealing with 124–6
  types 121–2
  wildlife gardening 95
  worst 126–7
west-facing walls 112
westerly winds 24
wigwams 59, 106, *110*
wildflowers 85, 91–2
wildlife gardening **84–96**
  at a glance 95–6
  birds 92–3

grass 91–2
insects 93–5
ponds 86–91
weeds 122, 127
willow:
  autumn 15, 17
  pruning 162
wind 19–20, **24–5**
  containers 107
  exotic gardens 80
  maple trees 60
winter 18–23, *38*
  colour 44
  exotic gardens 80
  landscaping 52
  plants that survive 22
  pruning 160, 162
  shrubs 116
  see also December; February;
    January
wisteria 69
  pruning 158
  supporting 112
woodlice 135
worms 27–8
  compost 140, 177, 206
  lawns 120
  moles 131
Writing Garden *35*, 45, *46*, 47

Y Z

yew 82, 163
  cuttings 248
yuccas 79, 81
zinnias:
  August 240
  colour 42
  June 232
  September 246
  summer 12

Picture Credits

All pictures by **Monty Don** except: **Alamy Stock Photo:** John Martin: p133; **Sarah Don:** p161;
Jason Ingram: p6, p29, p35, p55, p76, p87, p110, p151, p182, p194, p201, p202; **Derry Moore:** p2, p272

Author Biography

Monty Don has been gardening on TV for over 25 years for ITV, Channel 4 and the BBC, and since 2003 has been the lead presenter on BBC TV's Gardeners' World, which from 2011 has been filmed in his own garden in Herefordshire – Longmeadow.

He is a longstanding organic gardener and was President of the Soil Association from 2008 to 2017.

A prolific journalist and author, he was gardening correspondent for the Observer from 1994 to 2006 and has written a weekly gardening column for the Daily Mail since 2004. He has published 18 books, including his recent Sunday Times bestseller, Nigel: My Family and Other Dogs.

....

Acknowledgments

At Dorling Kindersley, Mary-Clare Jerram and Hilary Mandleberg have been enthusiastic, patient and endlessly helpful. Derry Moore and Jason Ingram have both taken wonderful photographs. My family, garden and dogs have suffered the usual neglect that any book strews in its wake with great forbearance. Above all, Alexandra Henderson guided, cajoled, encouraged and at times marshalled this book into being without ever losing good humour. To all, my sincere thanks.

....

 Penguin Random House

Senior Editor Hilary Mandleberg   **Senior Designer** Alison Shackleton

....

First published in Great Britain in 2017
by Dorling Kindersley Limited
DK, One Embassy Gardens, 8 Viaduct Gardens,
London, SW11 7BW

Text copyright © 2017 Monty Don
All pictures © 2017 Monty Don except:
p133 Alamy Stock Photo © 2017 John Martin;
p161 © 2017 Sarah Don; p6, p29, p35, p55, p76, p87,
p110, p151, p182, p194, p201, p202 © 2017 Jason Ingram;
p2, p272 and cover images © 2017 Derry Moore

Copyright © 2017 Dorling Kindersley Limited
A Penguin Random House Company
16 18 20 22 24 23 21 19 17 15
024–308224–October/2017

A CIP catalogue record for this book
is available from the British Library.
ISBN: 978-0-2413-1827-0

Printed and bound in China

For the curious
www.dk.com

for trunk of height – 6ft –
span – an arms stretch 5-4ft –
a pace – 3ft – a hands breadth
– 7 inches – 2 people walking
comfortably side by side – 5ft –
hip height about 3ft –
all these are useful and
important measurements

There is usually a knight's
moment to price any plan
but often the best time
is when you have the
~~cover~~ appropriate tool to hand, are
there and minded to do it.